Retrofitting for Quick Die Change in America

Gary Zunker
Lightning Time Savers

KENDALL/HUNT PUBLISHING COMPANY
2460 Kerper Boulevard P.O. Box 539 Dubuque, Iowa 52004-0539

Editor
Amy Boeselager

Graphic Artists
Sherry Young, Mary Rothkopf

Cover Design
Debra Strout

This edition has been printed directly from camera-ready copy.

Copyright © 1991 by Gary Zunker

ISBN 0-8403-6561-6

Printed in the United States of America
10 9 8 7 6 5 4 3 2 1

Contents

Acknowledgements

I would like to thank the salaried and hourly employees at John Deere - Horicon. In particular, I would like to thank Bob Downing, production supervisor, for his knowledge and his gung-ho attitude. Many times I heard him say, "Let's try it and see if it works. Let's be open-minded and try everything we can to **make** it work." I know that many of the equipment installations that I managed were looked down upon as possibly disastrous, but it is people like Bob Downing, who stood by me and worked with me, who helped to make these things happen successfully.

I hope that as other engineers take on new challenges, implementing new ideas and installing new equipment and hardware, they also find people like Bob Downing to work with them toward success.

Naturally, to be successful, you need upper management support. I would like to thank Dick Teal for his support at Deere and his willingness to listen and try new ideas. It is people like Dick who will ensure that this country will turn things around and become more competitive in the future.

I would also like to acknowledge the hourly employees at Deere, particularly John Moore, press operator; Marty Schraufnager, setup man; Rich Amerling, machine repairman; and Sam Harringa, electrician.

The people on the production floor deserve acknowledgement for their efforts in helping me make these equipment and die modifications a reality. I learned much working with them, and, above all else, they have taught me the importance of working with the people on the production floor. Through their knowledge, I became a better engineer and stayed on the straight path to success, avoiding many mistakes along the way.

Finally, I would like to express my gratitude to my clients over these past years who have put their faith in my company and have been willing to invest their time, monies, and manpower to work with me implementing quick die change. Their business is greatly appreciated, and I wish them nothing but the best in the future.

Introduction

There are over 60,000 stamping facilities in the United States. In the early 1980s, a new manufacturing strategy developed by the Japanese awakened American business to the fact that there is a different approach to how we should manage a business. Our challenge in America is that our stamping facilities must adapt new management techniques so that we can be competitive in the world marketplace.

This new approach has been called Just-In-Time Manufacturing. Just-In-Time (JIT) practitioners tell us that the theory behind JIT is that inventory hides inefficiencies, therefore contributing to higher manufacturing costs. To eliminate excess inventory, we must have the capability to produce efficiently in small lot sizes. Therefore, setups that used to take hours must now take minutes.

To accomplish the goal of reducing this existing job change time, two different alternatives are available:

1). Purchase new press equipment with quick change capability
2). Retrofit existing press equipment

This book addresses the second alternative and provides a step-by-step approach on how to retrofit to reduce setup time. It deals with the method, hardware, and tool modifications required to retrofit existing press equipment and bring about significant reductions in job change on both small and large presses.

Due to the constraints and limits of the book length, all available types of equipment cannot be covered. The author has chosen to discuss equipment which he has used and with which he has been successful. For complete information, consult the Thomas Registry, your trade association, trade publications, consultants, and vendors.

Die changeover time reductions of 70, 80, even 90 percent do not happen overnight. It takes many months to plan and years to implement quick die change programs. The most exciting thing about quick die change is that much can be accomplished using simple method changes, and significant savings can be readily seen as a result.

The savings is so outstanding that it motivates the implementer to go on to even greater results. As you become familiar with the material in this book, it will become apparent that quick change principles can be applied to a wide range of manufacturing operations from job shops to highly automated factories.

The author has chosen to discuss retrofit in this book versus the purchase of new equipment as a means of reducing setup time for the following reasons:

• Most companies do not have the capital to purchase new presses with quick change capability.
• Companies throughout the United States are looking for guidance on how to maximize their existing equipment before investing in new equipment.

• It is the most difficult approach:
  − Success is dependent on the engineering expertise within the company.
  − There is a long lead time. Implementation is a slow process.
  − Retrofitting requires a large commitment of manpower within the organization to accomplish the task.
  − Disruption of production during the implementation phase is possible.

The bottom line is that by retrofitting, a company will maximize the use of its existing equipment and lower labor and operating costs. This will result in improved competitiveness in the marketplace.

To address the issue of retrofitting existing presses to achieve minimum job change, the book is divided into seven parts:

Part One: Defines minimum job change and identifies its benefits.

Part Two: Identifies how to get started in developing your own program. It provides a step-by-step approach to implementing a quick change program.

Part Three: Describes how to identify costs involved in quick die change and how to compute savings.

Part Four: Explains how to reduce setup time through planning, standardization, and equipment.

Part Five: Describes how to choose a die handling system: what questions you need to ask and some of the types of equipment that are available.

Part Six: Describes actual applications of quick die change through the use of case studies.

Part Seven: Identifies the requirements for readying the die before and after job change to achieve single digit die change times.

The information in this book is based on proven ideas and hardware introduced in an actual production environment. Many of these ideas can be applied in any press shop and on any press to reduce setup time.

The objectives of this book are to:

• Identify the various steps required to implement quick die change, focusing on how to perform the change rather than why it should be done.
• Explain some of the various hardware and method improvements that are available.
• Explain how to standardize to eliminate press and tool adjustments.
• Explain how to justify your quick die change system.
• Explain some of the equipment that is available to ready the die before and after the die change.
• Expose the reader to new technology, including:
  − A state-of-the-art die changer for dies weighing 5,000 to 40,000 pounds.
  − A fully automatic exchange of dies in a press in two minutes.
  − A state-of-the-art die manipulator. Reduction in setup time in the press area has led to a new generation of die handling equipment for die maintenance.

— Equipment that will automatically open, wash, and close 8,000- to 40,000-pound dies in less than 12 minutes.

Please note that some of the photographs and drawings in this book may be printed with safety equipment removed. However, in actual operation, it is recommended that correct safety procedures and equipment be used.

The Croydon Group, Ltd., Fabricators and Manufacturers Association, International, and Lightning Time Savers assume no liability in connection with reader utilization of the information contained herein.

What is Minimum Job Change?

1

Minimum job change time is the time required for a process changeover. It is continually driven toward zero and is a key element to the Just-In-Time philosophy.

The object of this philosophy is to eliminate waste. JIT is the supply of only the necessary parts, in the necessary amount, at the necessary time and place. The philosophy is that inventory hides manufacturing wastes and is, therefore, the **worst** waste. Success or failure of a JIT system is dependent upon the success of minimum job change. In order to reduce lot sizes significantly, the press department supplying parts must be able to react to the immediate demand for different part families at minimum inventory.

A quick die change system is more than a method that significantly reduces the downtime on your presses from hours to minutes; it is a new manufacturing strategy that drives the factory to eliminate production wastes and, therefore, improve its overall competitiveness.

JIT manufacturing is based on the premise that the largest factor contributing to shop inefficiency is inventory. The cost of storing, maintaining, controlling, and financing inventory is the largest contributor to a company's production costs. Therefore, if you reduce inventory through quick die change, productivity and quality will be increased, lowering overall factory costs.

In **Figure 1**, a two hour setup results in higher inventory (20 day bank) and the cost of manufacturing a unit increases. Reducing the changeover time to an hour results in a 10-day lot size and lower production. In other words, a reduction in setup time will result in a reduction in the economic lot size and lead to a lower unit cost.

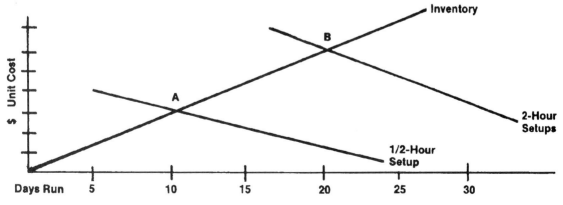

Figure 1: Reduction in setup time

The effects of quick die change can be likened to a body of water. When the level is high, submerged obstacles are hidden. When the body of water is lowered, "rocks" surface.

In manufacturing, we build inventory Work in Process (WIP) because we have problems in the processing of parts. Such problems may include scrap, poor weldments, fitup problems, scheduling, and delays between operations, tool maintenance, etc. If we take away the WIP inventory between the operations, we are forced to confront these problems and find solutions.

The end result is that quick die change becomes the compelling force to make our processes more efficient, because we no longer have the inventory lying around to bail us out. Previously, large amounts of inventory made many of our problems seem insignificant, so the problems were overlooked. Deliberate reduction in that inventory reveals our problems. Finding solutions makes us more efficient and more competitive. Quick die change becomes the force that drives us to continue to seek new ways to solve our problems.

The opportunities that quick die change and JIT manufacturing present to our country are exciting. We as a nation are facing the toughest competition in our history.

In fact, the May 21, 1990, issue of USA TODAY reported on a town meeting between an official from Japan and retired automakers, union leaders, and politicians. At the meeting, the attendees agreed on the sorry state of U.S. factories not being able to compete with Japanese goods. "We have a lot of soul searching to do and action to take" said Rep. Sander Levin, D-Mich. meeting organizer,[1] commenting on what it will take for the U.S. to become competitive again.

Shintaro Ishihara, a candidate for Prime Minister of Japan, is coauthor of the book, The Japan That Can Say No.[2] In the book, he brands the USA a giant crybaby that cannot figure out how to compete. At the meeting, Mr. Ishihara said that the U.S. can bounce back and regain its economic muscle, but America must revive its American industry.

We need American management to begin planning for the future, looking at long term manufacturing strategies using quick die change JIT techniques to reduce manufacturing costs and improve part quality. Only then can we regain our competitive edge and again compete with the Pacific and European countries.

There is more at stake than just immediate markets. This is a race toward the future for ourselves and our children. If the United States loses its competitive edge, we will face fewer good jobs, shrinking incomes, and a declining standard of living. So, America, let's get started!

[1]Copyright 1990, USA TODAY. Excerpted with permission.
[2]Akio Morita and Shintaro Ishihara

How To Get Started

Although there are definite steps to be followed to get your quick die change program started, there are some preliminary actions that must be taken. First, you must have backing from your top management. Top management must be supportive and provide both funding and manpower for accomplishing the task. The next step is to organize a steering committee of second level management. The committee would administer the project and control spending and manpower expended to complete the task.

The steering committee would consist of department heads from:

- Process & tool engineering
- Manufacturing
- Industrial engineering
- Production control
- Maintenance
- Accounting

Figure 2 presents an organizational flow chart for implementing quick die change. This particular chart was used at a stainless steel sink manufacturer in Wisconsin.

Once the preliminaries have been accomplished, you can follow these steps toward quick die change implementation.

Step One: Selecting the Team

Often, the most effective means to manage any large project is through team participation. The team approach carries many advantages.

Talent can be drawn from different departments, and the cooperation from the department heads is enhanced when they are represented on the team. Also, when a consensus is obtained from all team members, more sound decisions are made. Group support of those decisions makes your ideas more saleable.

With the team approach, lines of authority are not permanent. There is less concern about pleasing a particular person, so more attention can be given to the end result. However, to head the team, you must have a project manager. He is responsible for the specific project, coordinates the work of the team, and reports back to the management on the status of the project.

When selecting team members, do not forget to incorporate shop expertise. The production supervisor of the area being affected should be included. Production people from the floor who are being affected, such as production operators and the setup man, should also be a part of the team, as should engineering personnel, including industrial engineers and process and tool engineers.

Additionally, representatives from the various support departments should be incorporated into the team. These departments may include tool room, tool crib, die storage, maintenance, and material handling.

If we as a nation are going to improve our competitiveness, we must better use our resources. One of those resources is the hourly labor force. The following was hung on the

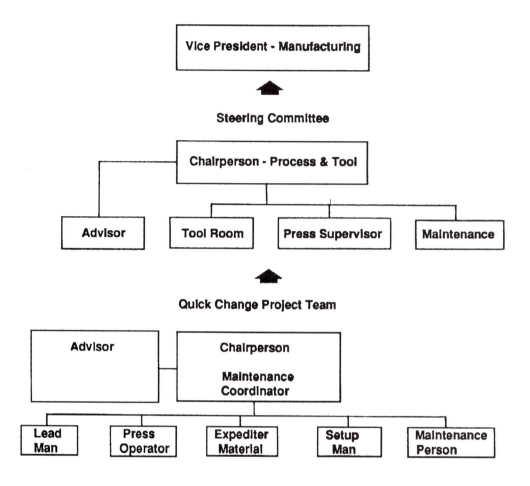

Figure 2: Organizational flow chart for quick die change implementation

door of the office of the manager of engineering at a Japanese firm:

"We (Japanese) are going to win and the industrial west is going to lose out. There is nothing much you can do about it, because the reasons for your failure are within yourselves. Your firms are built on the (Fredrick) Taylor model, where your bosses do the thinking while your workers yield the screwdrivers. You're convinced, deep down, that this is the right way to run a business."

If we are to succeed, the barriers between management and employee must be removed. Why do we need the participation of hourly employees in order to be successful?

• **To win acceptance from the people on the floor**. Resisting change is a common reaction. If the people being affected by the change were able to contribute and be a part of the decision-making process, then resistance would be minimal.

• **Objectives will be more realistic.** Objectives from a participative atmosphere tend to be realistic and more imaginative because they have been created with the help of a cross section of people close to the problems. They know what the real problems are because they live with them every day, about 232 work days each year.

• **They will make significant contributions.** Approximately 60 percent of all the ideas and method changes discussed in this book came from the hourly people on the floor. These ideas include preassembled die clamps, prestaging dies, T-slot bolsters, and die positioning using pins in the bolster.

• **They will take ownership and become involved in ensuring that the equipment will be maintained and used.**

This last point can be illustrated more fully with a comparison of employee participation in the start-up of two new die carts. One cart was built with no input from hourly maintenance employees.

Hourly maintenance people **were** involved during the building of the second cart, including visiting the vendor during the build stage. The vendor took the following actions as a result of recommendations made by the hourly maintenance employees:

1. **Increased serviceability**
   • Hydraulic manifolds were moved closer to point of use.
   • Quick change control lines were added.
   • Use of nylon air tubing, which is rated at four times the pressure as the original tubing in the first cart, was recommended. This reduced the chance of air lines blowing off, which was experienced with the first cart.
   • More space was added around the drive wheel so that a wrench could be used for adjusting chain tension.

2. **Improved overall performance**
   • Air chambers were added between air bearings and flow control valves to reduce hopping (caused by a large influx of air to the bearings) and flat tires when driving, a result of air fluctuations.
   • Colored indicator lights were added to the control console to reduce operator error when operating push/pull arms.
   • Additional air chambers were added to reduce the time needed to inflate air bearings from 30 to 15 seconds. This in turn reduced overall die exchange time to 115 seconds.

3. **Reduced startup problems**
   • The electrician discovered that there was insufficient space in the storage compartment for the PC controller to plug in the PC readout for troubleshooting. Had he not participated at the vendor, this problem would not have been discovered until after the cart was in-house.
   • The electrician also discovered errors in the existing program language. For instance, limit switches were not activating to ensure contact.

The inclusion of maintenance personnel at the vendor was advantageous. The employees could see the quality of the workmanship before the cart was assembled. This contributed to their buying ownership of the cart and their eagerness to make the cart a success. They also could see the interacting of the various components and controls. The employees initiated several modifications which would reduce start-up delays at the facility.

Following the trip, the maintenance personnel seemed to take responsibility for the cart. When it arrived at the facility, they were eager to work on the machine. In fact, they met the transport truck, unloaded the die cart, and moved it to its location. The lead time to start up the new cart was reduced by five work days as an end result.

Step Two: How to Get Started

The next step involves selecting a part or product for quick die change. First, you must select a particular product family that would make a significant impact on company costs. Once the product family is chosen, select one press or two similar presses out of a particular press group. Once the press or presses are chosen, you must look at all the tooling that runs across those presses.

All die sizes and weights should be compiled to determine die revisions required to standardize for die clamping and die exchange. You must plan to convert all tooling that runs across those presses for quick die change. This will guarantee uniformity and eliminate damage to quick die change hardware.

Finally, select a press and product group with which success is self-assured. Select a press group with which:

• Tool revisions to standardize will require a minimum amount of expenditures and lead time.

• Press operators are open to change and willing to be involved in the process to bring about change.

• Press location within the plant is advantageous to adding prestaging of the die set and the use of die carts to load and unload press dies.

• The maintenance and overall condition of the press will minimize expenditures

to convert the press for quick die change (T-slotted bolsters and ram, quick dump for lowering cushion pins, die clamping, etc.).

• Present traffic patterns around the presses for die and material flow will aid prestaging material and dies for quick die change.

Having an instant success provides the momentum to continue the program and motivate the employees on the production floor to support the quick die change effort.

Step Three: Selecting Your Goals

Goals must be selected and determined for your quick die change implementation. In doing so, basic project management skills must be used to get started. You must have clearly defined goals and a manufacturing plan of action or strategy that will enable you to complete your goals. When determining your goals, take into account what must be accomplished. These goals can be short and long range in scope. Short range involves less than one year to achieve, whereas long range goals may take two to three years to complete, and possibly longer.

Acceptable objectives can be defined with the following criteria. They must be:

• Clearly defined and measurable
• Supported by management
• Realistic and attainable
• Based on available or attainable resources

To ensure that the objectives are readily accepted, the people who have to do the work to meet the objectives should also take part in creating them.

Figure 3 shows a plan of action that was developed for a manufacturer of stainless

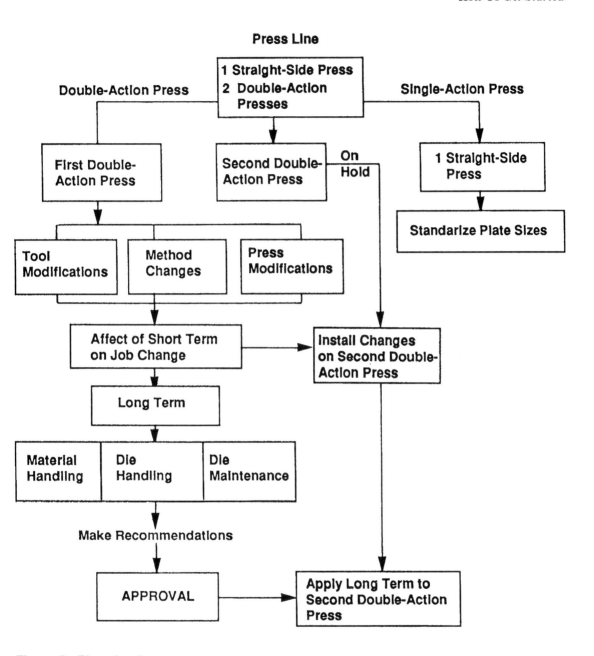

Figure 3: Plan of action

steel sinks. The company's plan was to retrofit one double-action press first. If successful, it would apply the same technology on the second press. These presses were chosen as the pilot to prove out planned press and die modifications for quick die change. If successful, the modifications would be used throughout the factory on 10 additional presses.

Step Four: Managing Time and Manpower

Once a plan of action is developed, the next step is to further break down the project into logical subunits. This allows the project manager to assign responsibilities and clearly understand the actions necessary to complete the objectives. A work breakdown structure must outline events and activities; detail the division of labor required from the various support departments; provide a structure for reporting the project status; and be used as a communicating device between the project team and management.

Project schedules can be used to develop this breakdown of subunits of work. Two types of project schedules are Gantt charts and critical path charts.

Gantt Charts. The first type of Gantt chart is a bar chart (see **Figure 4**). The figure shows the project schedule of a company whose goal was to install die rollers in a press bolster. Task 1 shows the company's time frame for ordering die rollers from the vendor, while Task 2 involves machining the bolster for die rollers. The time frame for delivering the rollers to the plant and installing the rollers is seen in Tasks 3 and 4.

When developing a Gantt bar chart, list activities along the vertical line and the activ-

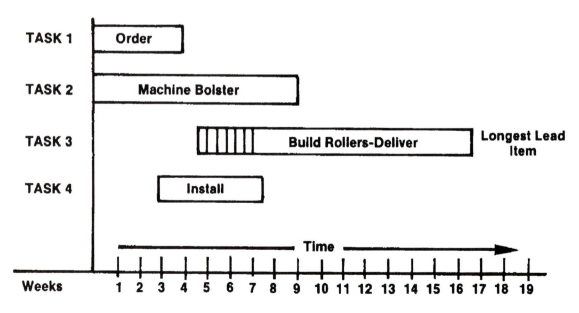

Figure 4: Gantt bar chart

ity schedule dates along the horizontal line. Next, estimate the duration of each activity and, using an outlined rectangle, draw each bar from the corresponding activity to the time of its duration. This is indicated by terminating the bar at its corresponding scheduled date. Activity progress to date (Task 3) should be indicated by filling in the portion of the bar corresponding to the approximate level of progress attained by the present day's position on the schedule.

The second type of Gantt chart is a milestone chart. It describes points in time when various items or activities are complete or available, but it does not show interrelationships between the various tasks with regard to when one task ends and the next task is to follow. **Figure 5** uses triangles to demonstrate the length of time for an activity or

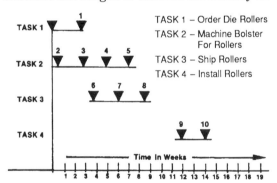

Figure 5: Gantt milestone chart

task. The tasks here are the same as in the bar chart example in Figure 4.

As any method of project scheduling, Gantt charts have advantages and disadvantages. The charts are simple and easily understood, as well as easily changed. They clearly show elements that are ahead or behind schedule. However, they do not show the interrelationships between tasks. Addi-

tionally, they do not show the complete story behind how all the various tasks are being completed.

Both Gantt bar and milestone charts are good techniques for smaller projects. They are not recommended where there is a large number of tasks and a need to show their interrelationships.

Critical Path Charts. The second main type of project schedule is a critical path chart (see **Figure 6**). In this chart, each line represents a defined task with a clear beginning, end, and time requirement. Each circle represents a completed task. So, for example, the allotted time to complete Task A in Figure 6 is two weeks.

The arrangement of the circles is significant. As shown, B is dependent of A; it cannot start until A is complete. In turn, C cannot start until B is done. Time required for the project is dependent on the longest path. In this case, A-E-F-G is the critical path.

Figure 7 shows a more complicated version of a critical path chart, used to explain the implementation phase for a quick die change project. This project was broken up into two major parts. Part One was the equipment and tool modifications required to retrofit one double-action press. Part Two was the design and build of a die cart system.

Step Five: Communicating Results

Finally, feedback must be provided to upper management on the status of your project team. To accomplish this, set up periodic management reviews. Dates for these reviews should be strategically designated about every three months to provide periodic updates. They should occur when significant milestones or objectives have been accom-

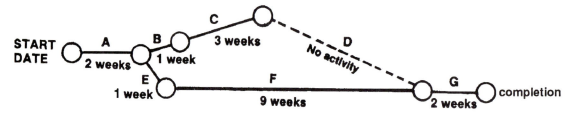

Figure 6: Simple critical path chart

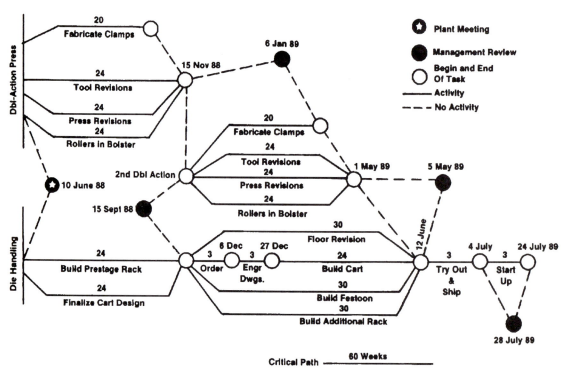

Figure 7: Complex critical path chart

plished. In these reviews, you should include the status on meeting certain dates or milestones. You should also discuss money expenditures.

These reviews present a chance to inform management at an early stage of any significant problems that cannot be overcome by the project team. Use the time to solicit their help in removing those road blocks. In addition to setting up periodic management reviews, also be sure to reissue updated project schedules to team members and upper management. This will keep everyone informed and concentrating on your project team's activities.

10

Justifying Quick Die Change

3

To be successful in justifying and implementing quick die change, we must stop looking only at direct labor. When a team of engineers from one U.S. manufacturing company visited several plants in Japan, they were awakened to a new approach to looking at manufacturing costs. In America, our traditional method of reducing manufacturing costs is to attack direct labor. We look at direct labor as being a large portion of the total manufacturing cost. In reality, as the Japanese have pointed out, direct labor is a very small portion of our total manufacturing costs. The true costs, or burden, are:

- Equipment underutilization
- Work in progress (WIP)
- People
  - Production schedulers
  - Storekeepers
  - Quality inspectors
  - Industrial engineers
  - Accounting clerks
- Outsource
- Material handling
- Scrap, rework
- Direct labor doing indirect work
- Excessive layers of supervision

At a typical stamping company, the above burden may make up approximately 50.9 percent of its total manufacturing costs, while material comprises 44.1 percent and labor a mere 5 percent. However, when companies attack these costs, they often do so as though labor comprises 75 percent of the costs, thinking that burden and material make up only 15 and 10 percent, respectively.

Identifying All Costs

How can quick die change be justified? First, you must look at "the big picture," including all costs associated with setup. Once inventory is reduced, you must address certain topics. These include the salaried work force; direct labor; indirect labor; WIP inventory; material handling; tool maintenance; part throughput, flow, and inspection; machine use; building space; and scrap rework.

Identifying and examining these topics gives you a road map for eliminating waste and reducing manufacturing costs.

Computing Savings

After identifying all costs, you must calculate your savings. Savings can be realized with regards to setup reduction/labor, inventory reduction, increased press use, and other savings. The following examples and calculations are actual savings realized after implementing quick die change.

Figure 8 shows the setup reduction/labor savings for two 500-ton presses. Here, setup time was reduced by two hours. You must take into account indirect labor cost increases for performing work previously performed while the press was down. This cost should be subtracted from the overall savings.

BEFORE	AFTER
130-Minute Job Change	10-Minute Job Change
1.5 People	2.0 People
6 Changeovers/Day	18 Changeovers/Day
232 Workdays/Year	232 Workdays/Year
= $113,000/Year	= $35,000/Year
Labor + Fringe	Labor + Fringe
	$113,000 - $35,000 = $78,000 Net Savings Per Year

Figure 8: Setup reduction/labor savings

Figure 9 demonstrates the savings resulting from inventory reduction on two 500-ton presses. According to the accounting department at the company where this quick die change was implemented, the cost reduction can be claimed for one year savings only. Your own finance department should be consulted to arrive at the savings for your company.

The savings from increased press use is seen in **Figure 10**. It shows the percentage of time and real hours, before and after the quick die change, spent in downtime, uptime, and changeover time. It also shows the cost of manufacturing savings and cost avoidance due to increased press capacity.

Savings can also be realized from other sources in a variety of areas. First, savings can be realized in lower WIP inventories. At one producer of lawn and garden equipment who implemented quick die change, 9,800 square feet of space (at $40 per square foot) was freed up. Additionally, there was no longer a need for indirect labor to move this material.

Second, savings can be realized from an increase in productivity. The production supervisor at the lawn and garden equipment company has realized 35 percent more production from his presses with the same manpower after gaining quick die change capability.

Third, scrap reduction results in savings. The same production supervisor has seen a 30 percent reduction in scrap and reject material since quick die change was implemented. In addition, on-site inspectors to check the operator's work were replaced with spot checks made at the material marshalling area.

Fourth, there is improved safety. Dies are now moved under control via die carts at the company during die exchange. Dies move smoothly in and out of the press bolster and prestage storage racks. Fork trucks or large bed die trucks are used outside the press area while production is running.

For instance, the author was consulting for a company in Missouri which asked to have its own die change videotaped. When the video was shown to employees, they witnessed on film a fork truck which had to slam on its brakes in a congested area, causing the die to roll off the forks and onto the floor. This type of occurrence causes damage to the die and can result in serious personal injury. Obviously, the elimination of such practices re-

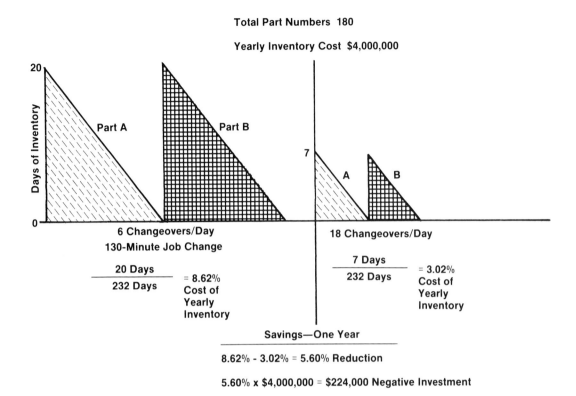

Figure 9: Inventory reduction/savings

sults in savings in worker's compensation and die repair.

In another instance, an automotive stamping company was performing die exchange with a flat bed die truck. To change the die, the driver would let the die slide off the truck into the press. He would then take a running start with the truck and slam into the die to push it in. It is not surprising that at this company, die trucks were always in repair, and dies were damaged. The important thing to remember is that die change cannot just be quick—it must be safe and easy as well.

Fifth, there is an opportunity for small batch deliveries to the assembly area, and this results in savings. Material handling labor is saved, as well as space for the storage of material.

Finally, housekeeping is improved (there is less congestion around presses) and fewer support personnel are needed, such as schedulers, stock chasers, clerks, supervisors, and inspectors. Intangible savings can also be included in the "other" category. These can come from using an untapped resource, such as ideas from the hourly production people.

	BEFORE			AFTER	
	%	**HOURS**		**%**	**HOURS**
DOWN 	5%	1.2		2.5%	0.6
RUN 	68%	16.3		91%	21.9
CHANGEOVER	27%	6.5		6.5%	1.5
		130 Minutes 3/Day			10 Minutes 9/Day
TOTAL		24.0			24.0
		68% UTILIZATION			91% UTILIZATION

21.9 - 16.3 = 5.6 Additional Press Hours For Production

5.6 Hours x 232 Work Days/Year = 1,299 Hours/Year

1,299 Hours x $100 (Cost/Machine/Hour) = $129,900 Yearly Savings

or

$$\frac{\$129,900}{\$450,000} \quad \frac{\text{Manufacturing Savings}}{\text{Cost For a New 950-Ton Press}} = \text{3/10 Price Of New Machine Cost Avoidance}$$

Figure 10: Increased press use/savings

When actually calculating costs, a very important ingredient in successfully developing your cost justification is an accountant from your financial department. Include him or her on the work team. Having an accountant on the team can help reduce lead time in developing costs versus savings. Who is more qualified and has access to cost figures for material and burden than your accountant? How many times has a project been held up until the financial people have reviewed the project and given approval?

By involving the accountant up front, he is familiar with your costs and savings calculations. He is aware what your team is trying to accomplish. Additionally, with an accountant on the team, credibility is established early that this is an acceptable project. The accountant will have an understanding of the costs and savings, and present corporate climate for approving this type of project. Therefore, you will know up front if this project has a chance of approval before you have expended a great deal of time and energy.

Figure 11 shows an example of a savings calculation worksheet which can be used to determine the amount of tangible savings you can expect by implementing quick die change. This will help to determine if quick die change is the right option for you, and, if it is, to convince accounting or higher management of quick die change's benefit to your company.

Savings Calculations Worksheet

Tangible Savings

1) **Reduced Labor For Setups**

   Before:

   $$\overline{\text{Mins./}} \quad \text{x} \quad \overline{\text{No. Of}} \quad \text{x} \quad \overline{\text{No. Of}} \quad + \quad 60 \text{ Mins.} \quad = \quad \overline{\qquad}\text{Hrs.}$$

   | Mins./ Changeover | | No. Of Changeovers/Day | | No. Of People | | 60 Mins. | | Hrs./Day For Changeover |

   $$\overline{\text{Hrs./Day}} \quad \text{x} \quad \overline{\substack{\text{Work Days} \\ \text{In A Year}}} \quad \text{x} \quad \overline{\substack{\$ \\ \text{Hourly Labor} \\ \text{Rate}}} \quad = \quad \overline{\substack{\$ \\ \text{Projected} \\ \text{Yearly Cost}}}$$

   After:

   | Mins./ Changeover | | No. Of Changeovers/Day | | No. Of People | | 60 Mins. | | Hrs./Day For Changeover |

   $$\overline{\text{Hrs./Day}} \quad \text{x} \quad \overline{\substack{\text{Work Days} \\ \text{In a Year}}} \quad \text{x} \quad \overline{\substack{\$ \\ \text{Hourly Labor} \\ \text{Rate}}} \quad = \quad \overline{\substack{\$ \\ \text{Projected} \\ \text{Yearly Cost}}}$$

   Projected Savings:

   $$\overline{\substack{\$ \\ \text{Before} \\ \text{Yearly Cost}}} \quad - \quad \overline{\substack{\$ \\ \text{After} \\ \text{Yearly Cost}}} \quad = \quad \overline{\substack{\$ \\ \text{Yearly} \\ \text{Savings}}}$$

Figure 11: Savings calculation worksheet

2) <u>**Inventory Reduction (One Year Savings)**</u>

Before: $\dfrac{\text{Present Day Bank}}{\text{Yearly Work Days}}$ = _____ % Cost of Inventory

After: $\dfrac{\text{Proposed Day Bank}}{\text{Yearly Work Days}}$ = _____ % Cost of Inventory

$$\underset{\substack{\text{Yearly Cost Of} \\ \text{Inventory (All} \\ \text{Parts That Run} \\ \text{On Press)}}}{\$\underline{\hspace{2cm}}} \quad \text{x} \quad \underset{\substack{\text{Difference} \\ \text{Between} \\ \text{Before \&} \\ \text{After}}}{\underline{\hspace{2cm}}\%} \quad = \quad \underset{\substack{\text{Negative} \\ \text{Investment} \\ \text{In Inventory}}}{\$\underline{\hspace{2cm}}}$$

3) <u>**Savings From No Farmout**</u>   <u>**Machine Hours Saved**</u>

Before:

$$\underset{\substack{\text{No. Of} \\ \text{Changeovers/Day}}}{\underline{\hspace{2cm}}} \text{ x } \underset{\substack{\text{Mins. For} \\ \text{Changeover}}}{\underline{\hspace{2cm}}} \text{ + 60 Mins. x } \underset{\substack{\text{No. Of} \\ \text{Work Days}}}{\underline{\hspace{2cm}}} = \underset{\substack{\text{Yearly} \\ \text{Machine Hrs.}}}{\underline{\hspace{2cm}}}$$

After:

$$\underset{\substack{\text{No. Of} \\ \text{Changeovers/Day}}}{\underline{\hspace{2cm}}} \text{ x } \underset{\substack{\text{Mins. For} \\ \text{Changeover}}}{\underline{\hspace{2cm}}} \text{ + 60 Mins. x } \underset{\substack{\text{No. Of} \\ \text{Work Days}}}{\underline{\hspace{2cm}}} = \underset{\substack{\text{Yearly} \\ \text{Machine Hrs.}}}{\underline{\hspace{2cm}}}$$

$$\underset{\text{Before}}{\underline{\hspace{1.5cm}}\text{ Hrs.}} \quad - \quad \underset{\text{After}}{\underline{\hspace{1.5cm}}\text{ Hrs.}} \quad = \quad \underset{\substack{\text{Machine Hrs.} \\ \text{Saved/Year}}}{\underline{\hspace{2cm}}}$$

$$\underset{\substack{\text{Yearly Machine} \\ \text{Hrs. Saved}}}{\underline{\hspace{2cm}}\text{Hrs.}} \quad \text{x} \quad \underset{\substack{\text{Per Hr. Cost} \\ \text{Above In House} \\ \text{Cost}}}{\$\underline{\hspace{2cm}}} \quad = \quad \underset{\substack{\text{Yearly} \\ \text{Farmout} \\ \text{Savings}}}{\$\underline{\hspace{2cm}}}$$

Figure 11: Savings calculation worksheet (continued)

Setup Reduction

4

Charts and Graphs for Planning

The first step in setup reduction is to analyze the existing setup time, or the time between when Part A has stopped running and Part B has started running. **Figure 12** demonstrates this setup reduction process.

First, simple method changes are installed. The first 50 percent reduction in job change can be quite easy with a minimum amount of expenditures. These reductions are the result of input from the production people on the floor and therefore require the least amount of time to implement. The last 40 to 50 percent reduction in setup time requires major press and tool revisions. This could result in major expenditures and long lead time for implementation.

Therefore, ongoing comparisons must continually be made between costs and setup reduction as you strive toward your goal of minimum setup time. What becomes "minimum" depends on how much money management wants to commit to reach zero setup time.

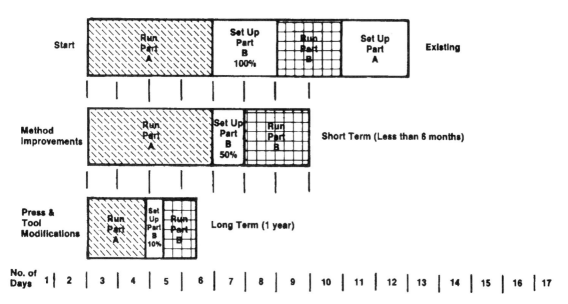

Courtesy of Joseph Papp

Figure 12: Analysis of existing setup time

Whether you are quick die changing a press, mill machine, drill press, or other machine, the following steps should be followed in implementing a successful quick die change program:

1. Identify elements
2. Breakdown internal/external elements
3. Reduce internal elements
4. Standardize to eliminate adjustments
   a. Tooling revisions
   b. Press modifications
5. Repeat process until goal is achieved

Two types of charts can be used to help your team analyze your present setup time and work toward reducing it.

First, to define your present setup time, the process chart in **Figure 13** will help you to define all the elements that make up the job change. This chart will provide good documentation for future use and will also define any bottlenecks because the biggest time elements are defined. To fill in the chart, review an actual die change and record all elements of time while the press is down. It can be recorded in seconds with a wristwatch, or it can be time studied with a stopwatch.

Second, after the process chart is filled out, plot the individual elements using a bar chart to prioritize according to time (see **Figure 14**). In the figure, Element 5 has the greatest amount of time. Therefore, a significant reduction in setup is possible if this element could be greatly reduced. By continuing to use the bar chart approach, you have a systematic way to continually reduce job change time. Repeat this process until you have met your objectives.

To aid in analyzing the bottlenecks in your present setup time, the use of a video camera should be employed. By recording die setup and change, the team will be able to visually review each element off-site. This will limit disruption on the production floor as you carry out your investigation.

Internal/External Time Elements

The second step in setup reduction is to break down all elements into internal and external time.

Internal elements are those elements of work that are performed while the press is stopped during the job change. Examples of internal elements are:

- Exchanging the die within the press.
- Asiding and positioning new cushion pins.
- Raising/lowering the press ram.
- Clamping/unclamping the die.
- Running and inspecting the first piece.
- Cleaning the press bolster.

External elements are work elements performed to expedite the die change while the press is still running production. Examples of external elements include:

- Prestaging the next die set near the press to be changed over.
- Obtaining a mechanical detail sheet and placing it with the die.
- Readying cushion pins with the next die.
- Prestaging finish and rough stock containers.
- Prestaging stock oilers and scrap tubs.

Page   of

Activity	Summary			
		No.	Time	Distance
_____	Clamping	____	____	____
_____	Adjustment	____	____	____
Chart Begins_____	Inspect	____	____	____
	Get-Find	____	____	____
Chart Ends _____	Other	____	____	____
Charted By____ Date ____	TOTALS	____	____	____

ELEMENTS OF WORK	C = Clamping A = Adjustment I = Inspect G = Get-Find O = Other					Time --Distance (Walk or Travel)
	C	A	I	G	O	___
	C	A	I	G	O	___
	C	A	I	G	O	___
	C	A	I	G	O	___
	C	A	I	G	O	___
	C	A	I	G	O	___
	C	A	I	G	O	___
	C	A	I	G	O	___
	C	A	I	G	O	___
	C	A	I	G	O	___

Figure 13: Setup process chart

Courtesy of Joseph Papp

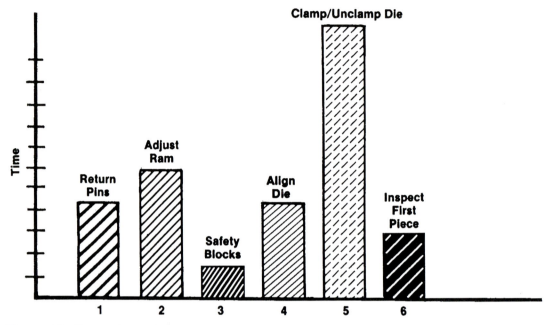

Figure 14: Setup elements

You may wish to introduce method changes to shrink the amount of direct labor required to perform these duties (see **Figure 15**). As shown in the illustration, the quantity of work performed by the direct labor person is reduced, and, consequently, the time the press is down for changeover is also reduced. Once you have identified those elements that can be performed outside the press while running parts, the work can be transferred to someone else.

For example, let us assume that, at present, the press operator is responsible for obtaining and positioning stock and scrap containers before and after each job change. The proposed transfer of work would assign that work to a setup man or stock chaser driver to ready stock and scrap containers. In many cases, you will find that in today's setup time, the press operator is waiting five to 10 minutes for the area fork trucker to bring the press operator his material. Because this wait time is considered unavoidable, it is included in the job change standard.

In another example, the operator may walk a long distance (100 feet) to obtain his job information sheets for running the next part. This element of work could take several minutes. The proposed transfer of work would involve reassigning this work to an indirect labor person (perhaps someone who works in the tool crib). This person would be responsible for gathering all the pertinent job information required to run the part and locate it with the die.

These examples may sound trivial, but these types of activities may be occurring daily in your press shop.

Standardize Press and Tooling

The third step in setup reduction is standardization—making dies and presses uniform to minimize time for setup. The project team goal here should be to standardize to eliminate all adjustments and shrink current time to perform all internal elements.

Two areas of concern in this standardization are tool revisions and press modification costs (these costs are based on averages for modifying 50 dies per press):

	75- to 250-ton	300- to 500-ton
Press	$90/ton	$90/ton
Tool	$104/ton	$200/ton

To estimate costs for these modifications and revisions, multiply the press tonnage by the cost-per-ton estimate for the press or tooling. For example, the cost to retrofit a 300-ton press with tooling at $200 per ton would be $200 x 300, or $60,000. This cost would cover subplating, standardizing clamping heights, and adding parallels to standardize shut height.

To minimize the number of adjustments related to the press tool, the following should be standardized:

- Die shoe clamping height
- Die shut height
- Adaptor plates
- Clamping devices
- Cushion pin lengths
- Die positioning

Die Shoe Clamping Thickness. When selecting a common bottom and top die shoe thickness, remember that it must be compatible with your clamping device. Also, the thickness should be the same for both the top and bottom die shoe.

For ease of clamping, two inches in from the edge of both the top and bottom die shoes should be free of obstructions along the entire surface (see **Figure 16**). This will aid the engineer in future retrofitting for adaptation to an automatic clamping system.

Shut Heights. If practical, standardize all dies so that they have a common shut height. This will eliminate the adjusting of the ram stroke before each new job change, saving approximately three to five minutes per job change, depending on die shut height.

To accomplish shut height standardization, buildup can be added to the bottom or top die shoe by adding risers (see **Figure 17**). Illustration I shows the process of adding risers to the bottom die shoe. When using this process, make sure that risers are located where they will not interfere with scrap shedding or cushion pin holes. Illustration II shows the process of adding risers to the top die shoe. Due to work height constraints, this may be the more advantageous choice of the two.

Shut height standardization allows no chance for operator error. However, disadvantages are found in lead time, the cost to revise the dies, and the tieup of engineering manpower to follow up on tool revisions. Building up your die sets to match a certain die shut height can also be expensive. An alternative would be to add to your press some type of mechanical method of automatically adjusting the press ram for the various die shut heights. This will be discussed in detail later.

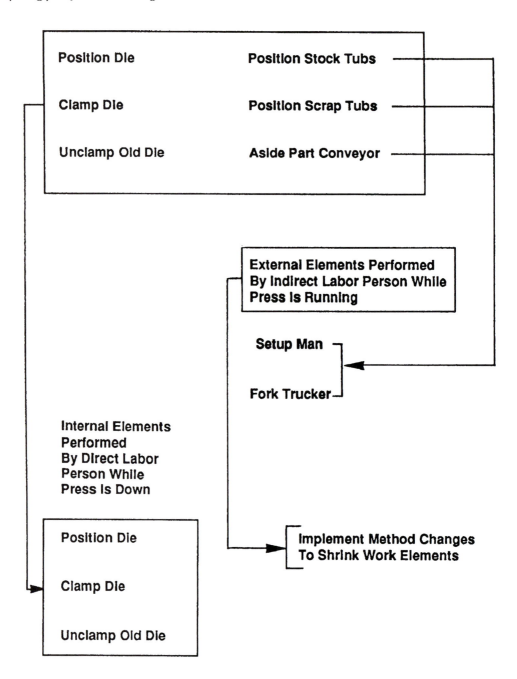

Figure 15: Internal elements performed by direct labor person while press is down

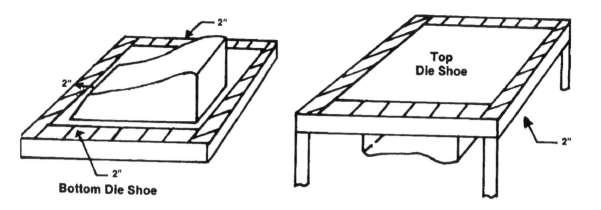

Figure 16: Clamping surface

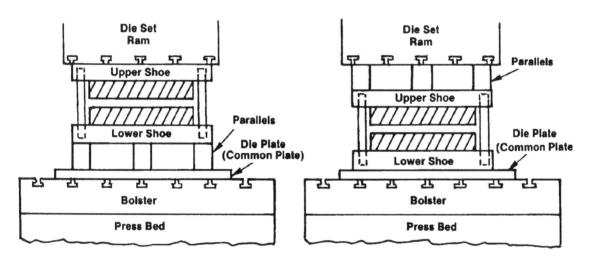

Figure 17: Die shoe buildup

Adaptor Plates. Adaptor plates can be used to standardize die widths and lengths. A common practice is to purchase blanchard ground plates which can be mounted to both the top and bottom die shoe. Thicknesses usually differ from one to three inches, depending on the size of the tooling and die weight.

There are a number of advantages of subplating, or adding adaptor plates to the top and bottom die shoe. The process:

• Provides a flat surface so the die can be rolled easily across the bolster.
• Gives the tooling a standard size (right to left and front to back).
• Provides a surface to which V-notch locator blocks for die positioning can be added.
• Provides a surface to which the die can be clamped, especially when adding automatic clamping.

• Provides a surface to trap scrap under the die during the production run. This will free the press bolster of slugs at the time of the job change.
• Provides an opportunity to join several single dies together to form one master die set (see **Figure 18**). This method reduces the quantity of presses, job changes, and manpower required to produce the part. When considering this option, look at the off-center loading that might occur on the press and the effect it will have on your existing die handling system. An alternative die handling

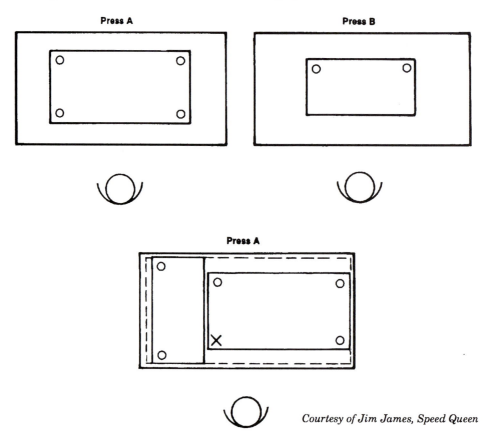

Courtesy of Jim James, Speed Queen

Figure 18: Combining operations of two dies on one master subplate

system might be required to handle the larger die weight.

• Reduces the number of die clamps required (see **Figure 19**).

Clamping Devices. Clamping devices are a concern in standardization. When new types of mechanical clamps are compared to hydraulic or air clamps, mechanical clamps are maintenance free and have no pump systems or hoses to install. Mechanical clamps have more clamping power as well. They do not drip oil as do hydraulic systems, and they bring about a 70 to 80 percent reduction in die clamping (at a much lower cost) as opposed to the conventional method (see **Figure 20**). However, as shown in Figure 20, a mechanical clamp system does not achieve the maximum result of the lowest possible time required for clamping.

The bottom line is that you can reduce your total die clamping/unclamping time by approximately two minutes with hydraulic/air clamping and an additional expenditure of approximately $15,000. Your team must decide what is the best clamping alternative for your dollar. Is two minutes for $15,000 more advantageous for savings, or can that $15,000 per press be used elsewhere to gain a larger return? For example, if you have five presses, hydraulic clamping would cost you an additional $75,000. If you decided against hydraulic clamping and purchased mechanical clamps at a lower price, the extra money could be used elsewhere to save even more time. The project team must decide where to spend the monies to obtain the best return.

There are a number of mechanical clamp types to consider. Only four types of these clamps will be discussed here. They are cheaper than the hydraulic clamps but do not save as much time. Of course, labor costs are present regardless of the choice. Keep in mind that one type of clamp is not always the answer.

One choice is the Optima mechanical clamp (see Figure 70, page 78). This type of clamp is manually operated, with no hydraulic or pneumatic components. Clamping force is obtained through the Toggle System design. Full pressure is achieved by turning the low torque "power nut" 180 degrees. It can be

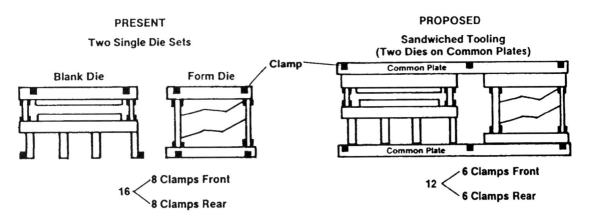

Figure 19: Reduction die clamp requirements

	Mechanical Clamps	Automatic Hydraulic/Air Clamping
Present Time In Job Change To Clamp & Unclamp (8 clamps) "Conventional Method"	**15 Minutes**	**15 Minutes**
Anticipated Time To Clamp & Unclamp After Installing New Clamp System (8 clamps) 1/2 Turn to Clamp & Unclamp	**3 Minutes**	**2 Minutes**
Estimated Cost Of The System	**$5,000**	**$20,000**

The above is based on using eight clamps; four clamps on both the top & bottom die shoe.

The costs are an average of several different size tonnage presses.

Figure 20: Mechanical clamps compared to automatic hydraulic/air clamping

easily inserted into existing T-slots, and positioning is simple, without additional fixing.

A second choice is the preassembled die clamp. For this type of clamp, simply weld the top of your existing T-bolt to form an individual clamp assembly (see **Figure 21**). With the old method, the operator had to assemble and reassemble die clamp pieces for the various clamp heights. With this method, clamp height is standardized so that the same clamp can be used over and over. The approximate cost is $300 per press. It carries the lowest cost and lead time in comparison to all other clamping devices on the market.

Another type of mechanical die clamp is a hand crank type (see **Figure 22**). This clamp can be permanently bolted to the press or easily removed using the optional T-slot nut. A large clamp has 8,750 pounds of clamping force. The clamp has a T-slot adaptor to fit in conventional 3/4-inch and 1-inch T-slots. The advantages of the hand crank type are that it

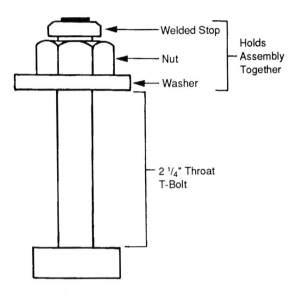

Figure 21: Preassembled die clamp

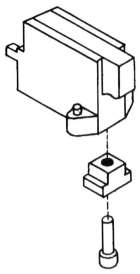

Courtesy of Forward Industries

Figure 22: Hand crank clamp

can fit into the existing T-slots mentioned above, and it generates substantial clamping force. However, the clamp robs space on the bolster plate. Additionally, hand cranking is not exacting. There is no readout to inform the operator that the desired clamping force has been made.

A fourth mechanical die clamp option is the boltless method (see **Figure 23**). This method is most widely used on small tooling (die weights less than 1,000 pounds). The operator positions the top and bottom individually in the press and uses an air wrench to tighten and untighten the holders.

Cushion Pin Lengths. If cushion pins are used, standardize their lengths whenever possible. However, to eliminate the need for cushion pins, it is recommended to investigate nitrogen cylinders in dies. The basic reasons for using nitrogen cylinders in dies are to obtain more force than is practical with springs, to obtain more travel, and to eliminate springs or cushion pins. Nitrogen die cylinder systems can be furnished as individual flange-mounted units connected to a reservoir tank, or self-contained packages mounted in a manifold plate (see **Figure 24**).

Nitrogen cylinders have a number of advantages over cushion pins. Nitrogen gas is not flammable, and it is easy to acquire. In addition, the cylinders eliminate:

• The use of pressure pins and press air cushions.
• Wait time during job change to lower cushion pins.
• The need to aside and position cushion pins during the job change.

There are, of course, disadvantages to nitrogen cylinder use. Not only must the reservoir tank be periodically recharged, but the estimated cost increase in the tool for adding

29

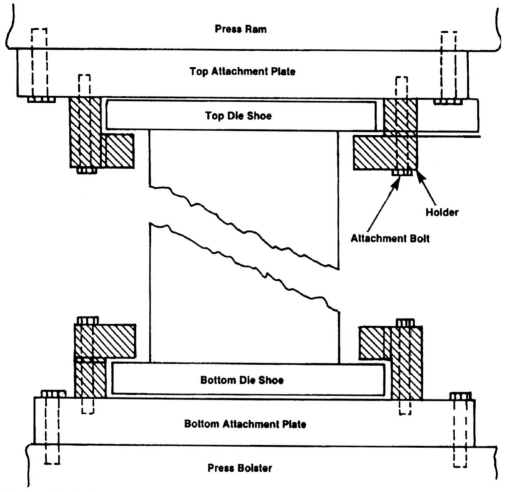

Figure 23: Boltless method

nitrogen cylinders is approximately $16,000 (average die size: 10 nitrogen cylinders per die, five-ton capacity). However, the present direction being taken in the automotive industry is to eliminate the use of all cushion pins. Therefore, more money is being spent up front on their tooling to use nitrogen cylinders.

It is recommended that, wherever possible, cushion pins should be eliminated. Cushion pins can add approximately eight minutes to the total job change time versus dies without cushion pins.

Die Positioning. Positioning devices should be considered as a means of centering the die inside the press. The simplest method for centering is to use some type of mechanical stops.

It should be considered that all dies that are run on the press have a consistent die

30

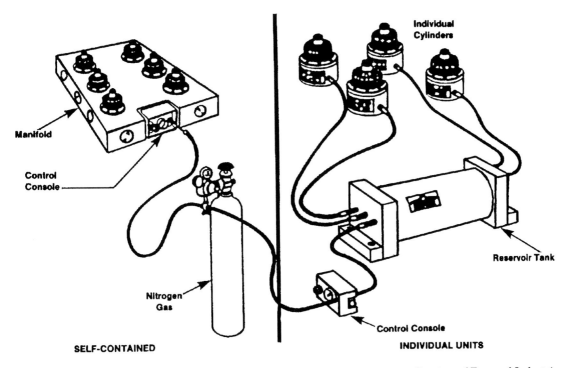

Manifold

Control
Console

Nitrogen
Gas

SELF-CONTAINED

Individual
Cylinders

Reservoir Tank

Control Console

INDIVIDUAL UNITS

Courtesy of Forward Industries

Figure 24: Nitrogen die cylinder systems: self-contained or individual

width and length. Where there are a large number of tools involved, select a minimum plate size that would work in conjunction with the die alignment pin locations. Also, consider adding some type of locating device to the rear or front of your dies, depending on the direction of die feed.

One widely used method for positioning dies on the press bolster is to add V-notch locators to the die set (see **Figure 25**). Illustration I shows the V-notch alignment lead welded to the side of the parallel or die shoe. Illustration II shows the V-block alignment lead welded to the base of the die plate. Shown in Illustration III is a milled V-notch in the die plate. These illustrations make up one full

size subplate, while Illustration IV shows multiple subplates.

Locating Pin Holes in the Bolster.
Usually, no more than one set of pin holes (equally distanced apart from the center) are used. The exceptions involve multiple pin hole locations. With coil feed presses, you must position various dies in several different locations on the bolster to align with the coil feeder. For cost reduction, you can reduce the overall size of the adaptor plate (front to back) to save on material and grinding costs.

Figure 26 shows the common method with two locating holes and the alternative method with multiple pin hole locations. Il-

31

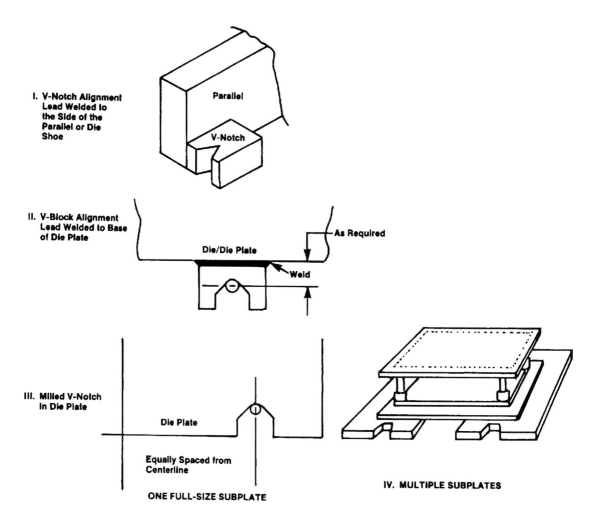

Figure 25: Adding V-notch locators to die set

lustration I is an example of a 500-ton large bed press (60 inches by 120 inches) with one set of location pins. In Illustration II, Die 1 is located on the pins farthest from the front of the press, while Die 2 is located on the pins closest to the front of the press. It shows a 6-inch reduction in overall die plate width (front to back).

After the die plate sizes have been established, you should then determine two locating points inside the bolster. These two points should be equally distanced from the press bed centerline.

Bringing it all together, **Figure 27** gives examples of aligning the die on the press bolster using removable stop-pins and V-notch

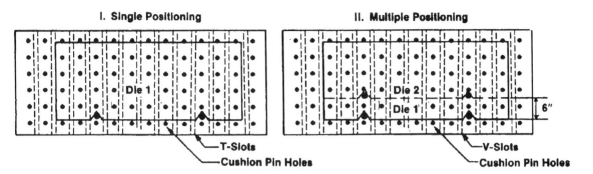

Figure 26: Positioning dies on press bolster with locating pins

die locators. In both examples, locator pins are equally distanced apart from the center of the press. Illustration II shows that the pins are staggered to eliminate the need for a second V-notch to reduce machining costs. This method is recommended for use on smaller press dies (less than 3,000 pounds).

Figure 28 shows multiple subplates being used on the same press. Here, the bolster of the large press is 60 inches by 120 inches. The minimum subplate size is 36 inches by 48 inches, the average subplate size is 48 inches by 84 inches, and the maximum subplate size is 60 inches by 120 inches. All sizes locate from the same locator pins which are equally distanced from the centerline of the press.

Standardize to Eliminate Press Adjustments

Various press modifications should be considered to reduce or eliminate press adjustments:

- Automatic ram adjustment
- Die rollers/lifter systems
- Machine bolster and ram
- Cushion quick dump
- Automatic die clamping versus manual

Automatic Ram Adjustment. An alternative to the expense of building up your die sets to match a certain die shut height would be to add to your press some type of mechanical method of automatically adjusting the press ram for the various die shut heights (see **Figure 29**). In this figure, the control panel is mounted to the press, fully programmed. It provides readout data and shows the preset ram position. The ram motor button engages the motor to raise and lower the ram. The encoder electronically knows where the ram is at all times. To set, the operator turns the thumb wheel to the desired setting and pushes the button to start the motor. When the ram reaches the desired setting, the operator hand-starts the inch mode to lower the ram to the die shoe.

The advantages of having an automatically adjusting ram are the cost (approximately $10,000) and the fact that no tool revisions are required. In addition, there is a shorter lead time to install versus the quantity of die revisions required, and there is less

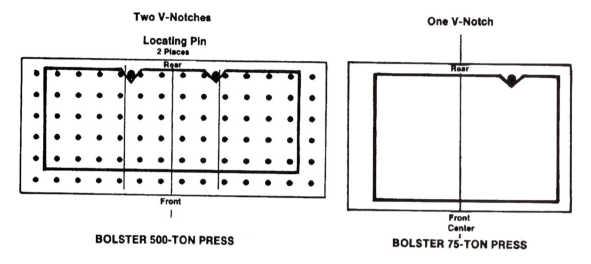

Figure 27: Positioning dies on press bolster with removable stop pins and V-notch die locators

disruption to the press shop. However, with this system, there is a chance for operator error.

Die Rollers/Lifter Systems. The most common aid for positioning a die on a press bolster is the use of die rollers/lifters. Why add die rollers? There is repeatability—the dies can be consistently centered in the press via the locating pins. Also, die rollers are safe because there are less pounds of force to horse in the die. For example, you need only 70 pounds of force to push/pull a 10,000-pound die.

With die rollers, there is no need for a pry bar and the back pains that accompany it. In addition, die rollers reduce the total job change time. From the author's experience, a job change time can usually be reduced by an average of 12 minutes with the use of die rollers. Speed is enhanced because to horse in the die with a pry bar is not required, and there is less friction.

Because die rollers raise the die 1/16 inch to 1/8 inch above the bolster, gouges in the bolster top caused by sliding the die over slugs laying on the bolster are eliminated. They allow the subplating of multiple die sets—the increased weight of several dies on one plate is easily maneuvered across the press bed with the aid of die lifters. Die positioning is also made easier because the rollers aid in aligning and pushing the die against the locating pins.

There are a wide variety of different rollers available. Three main types are ball bearing, roller bearing, and air float (see **Figure 30**). The ball bearing and roller bearing types both come with lift devices that may include coil spring, belleville washer, neoprene, and hydraulic types. The roller bearing type also comes with air-over-oil and pneumatic lift devices, while the air float type comes with just a pneumatic lift device.

In the ball bearing style, the roller ball is self-contained and rolls on individual ball

34

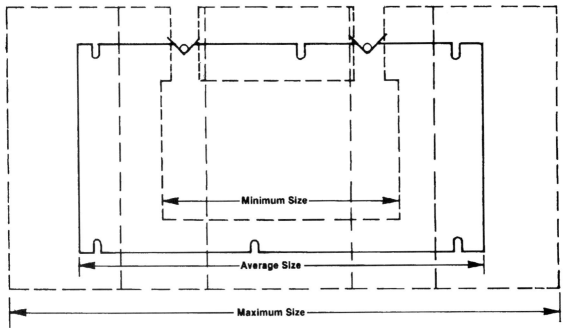

Courtesy of Jim James, Speed Queen

Figure 28: Multiple subplates used on the same press

bearings. The roller ball unit is lifted via springs or mechanical means via hydraulics. These can be individual single units placed on the bolster or mounted inside a rail. The roller bearing style is also self-contained. It rotates on an axle and travels within the machine pocket of the die rail. The complete rail (roller bearings included) is then lifted up or down by air or hydraulics.

Hydraulic and pneumatic lift types are shown in **Figure 31**. In the hydraulic lift, multiple cylinders do the up and down lifting. The pneumatic lift is rated to 500 PSI. The air bag is inflated with normal shop air (60 to 100 PSI) to raise and lower the rail.

Installation requirements range from no preparation (i.e. rollers fit into Joint In-

dustry Control (JIC) T-slots or mount on the top of the bolster), to bolster preparation which requires milling special slots. To aid the reader in comparing the most common die roller systems in the marketplace, a cost comparison for several die roller systems for handling 10,000- and 50,000-pound die weights is shown in **Figure 32**.

Of course, there are advantages and disadvantages to the different types of die rollers and lift devices. Ball bearing die rollers offer an excellent coefficient of rolling friction. This is estimated to be less than .004. In other words, a 1,000-pound die would require 4 pounds of force to move and roll the die. Additionally, they allow for free or multi-directional positioning of the die.

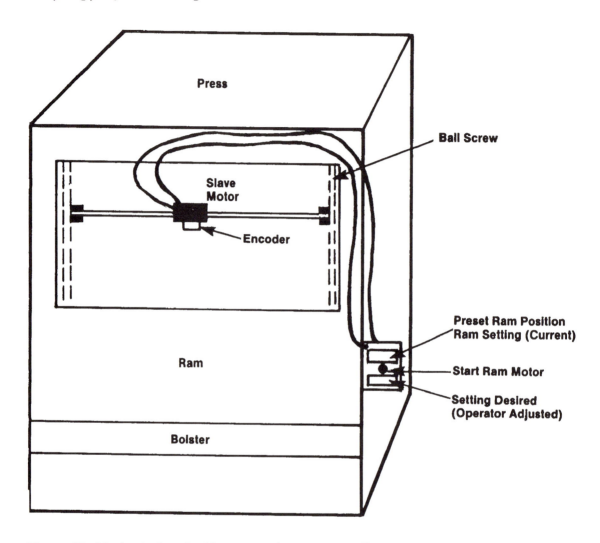

Figure 29: Mechanical method for automatic press ram adjustment

However, ball bearing die rollers have a low carrying capacity and require high maintenance because their design makes them susceptible to dirt, oil, and corrosion. The rollers tend to peen the die shoe because of the small contact surface. Many companies do offer special hardened strips which can be fastened to the subplates. Also, free positioning is not always desirable. For instance, if dies are prelocated and guided, single direction is desirable. Because of their limited carrying capacity, large amounts of bolster space are required for the installation of ball bearing die rollers.

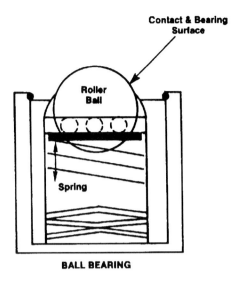

BALL BEARING

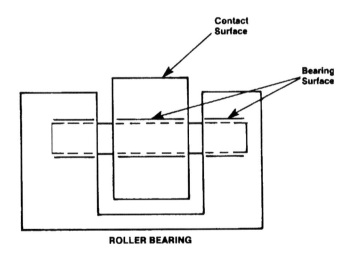

ROLLER BEARING

Figure 30: Die rollers: ball bearing and roller bearing

Roller bearing die rollers offer more capacity per linear foot, as much as three times more. They offer a good coefficient of rolling friction (.007). So, as illustrated in the ball bearing example, a 1,000-pound die would require 7 pounds of force to move and roll the die. They provide good guiding for single directional travel. Some companies offer a bi-

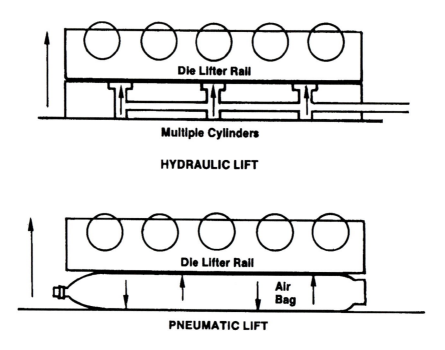

Figure 31: Lift types: hydraulic and pneumatic for raising/lowering die lifters

directional system in which a switch is used to raise and lower rollers in sequence in X and Y coordinates. Also, there is much less maintenance involved than with the ball bearing due to the design of the roller bearing.

The contact surface area of the roller bearing is approximately 10 times greater than that of the ball-style bearing (for crowned rollers). In addition, no special subplate hardening or preparation is required. However, roller bearing die rollers require more force to move the die. This was illustrated with the rolling friction calculations of .007 for the roller bearing versus .004 for the ball bearing. The roller bearing also does not allow as much freedom for die positioning as the ball bearing does.

The coil springs and belleville washer lift devices consume no energy and they are available at a low cost. However, these devices have a low lift capacity range, and maintenance is difficult. Also, spring force must be overcome by clamping.

The ball bearing die rollers may be used for weights less than 1,000 pounds in a "clean" environment where free positioning is desired. They may also be used for heavier weights (10,000 pounds), but, in this instance, hardening of the subplates should be performed. Applications of ball bearing die rollers include prestaging tables, small O.B.I. presses, tool room, and crib areas.

Roller bearing die rollers may be used for weights in excess of 1,000 pounds, especially in "unclean" areas. Some free positioning is available on crowned rollers and bidirectional systems. They are excellent for use with a guiding system. Applications of roller

A. 10,000 lb. Die (Using Ball Style Rollers)

Example

36" x 36" Bolster		Coil Spring		Neoprene
Lift Capacity/Ft.	— — —	845 Lbs.	— — — —	1800 Lbs.
No. Of Feet Reqd.	— — —	12'	— — — —	6'
Cost/Linear Ft.	— — —	$312.50	— — — —	$300.00
Total System Cost	— — —	$3,750.00	— — — —	$1,800.00
Price/Lb. of Lift	— — —	$0.38	— — — —	$0.18

B. 50,000 lb. Die (Using Roller Style Bearing)

Example

120" x 72" Bolster		Hydraulic Lift		Pneumatic Lift
Lift Capacity/Ft.	— — — — —	2490 lbs.	— — — —	2600 lbs.
No. of Ft. Reqd.	— — — — —	24'	— — — —	24'
Cost/Linear Ft.	— — — — —	$600.00	— — — —	$382.00
Roller Cost	— — — — —	$14,400.00	— — — —	$9,168.00
Additional	— — — — —	$750.00	— — — —	$293.00 (Hrdwre.)
			— — — —	$2,500 (Mill)
Total System Cost	— — — — —	$15,500.00	— — — —	$11,961.00
Price/Lb. of Lift	— — — — —	$0.30	— — — —	$0.24

Figure 32: Comparison of die roller systems

bearing die rollers are the same as those for ball bearing types, except that when using less than 1,000 pounds, the systems are oversized and not very cost-effective.

The coil spring and belleville washer lift devices may be used in "clean" environments with less than 1,000-pound die weights. The neoprene device can be used in "unclean" environments with temperatures less than 200 degrees F and die weights not exceeding 20,000 pounds. Weight ranges should be small, or removal of some rails may be required during setup.

Pneumatic lift devices are inexpensive to operate and have the best lift capacity. They can be used with dies weighing 1,000 pounds and over. Hydraulic lift devices have a good lifting capacity and are also to be used with dies weighing 1,000 pounds and over.

Machine Bolster and Ram. The JIC press users and manufacturers established standards for T-slot and cushion pin locations.

This standardization involves the use of letters for front to back locations and numerals for right to left locations. For example, in **Figure 33**, the location of the cushion pin is identified as A-4. With this, the operator knows that the cushion hole for the pin is in the front of the press (A) and is four holes over (4).

Cushion Quick Dump. A quick dump must be added for asiding air for cushion. An accumulator tank must be added to the press to reduce the time required for filling the cushion after each die change and to bleed off the air from the cushions. This air is then held in the accumulator and sent back to the cushions. This eliminates lengthy bleed off time (25 minutes average) when the cushions are bled off to the main air supply line.

Automatic Die Clamping Versus Manual. An alternative to hand and mechanical die clamping is to fully automate. In selecting a particular automatic die clamp

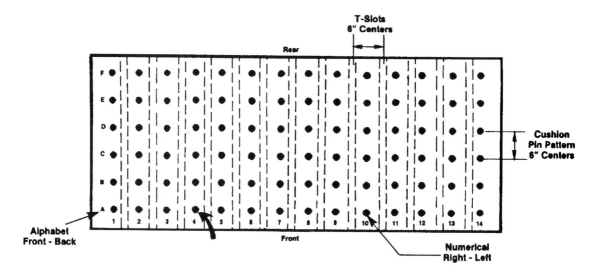

Figure 33: JIC standards for T-slot and cushion pin locations

system, the following should be considered:

- Selection of the die clamp
- Selection of the control system for safety
- Plumbing system design
- Clamping force desired for both top and bottom die shoe

In selecting a particular die clamp, the following should be considered:

- Die sizes in relation to the press ram and bolster
  - Is travel required before activating the clamp?
  - Are you going to clamp front to back or on the sides?
- Die shoe thickness
- Clamping force desired
- Availability of T-slots for clamping

<u>Manually Inserted</u>. The most widely used and least expensive die clamp is the manually-inserted T-bolt attached to an hydraulic cylinder. The T-bolt fits inside of the T-slot and is pressed up against the die shoe and locked in place (see **Figure 34**). The estimated cost to add this type of system to a press requiring eight clamps (60 inch by 60 inch press bed) is approximately $13,000. U cutouts will be required in the top and bottom die shoes for locating the die clamp onto the die shoe when using the T-bolt.

An alternative is to use a hollow cylinder (see **Figure 35**). This clamp is widely used for its large strokes and ease of positioning with different size dies.[3] Another alternative is a knuckle type (pivot) clamp (see **Figure 36**). The pivot arm rocks back and forth, energized hydraulically to engage and disengage.

<u>Permanently Positioned</u>. In addition to manually inserted clamps, you have the op-

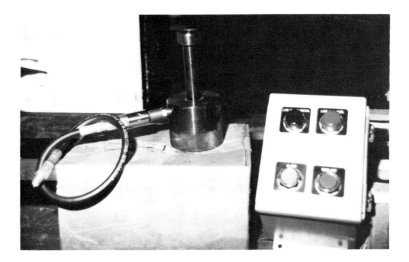

Figure 34: T-bolt hydraulic clamp and control panel box (Clamp capacity—10 tons per clamp)

---

[3]Enerpac Production Automation

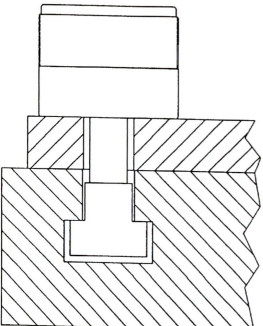

Courtesy of Enerpac Production Automation

Figure 35: Hollow cylinder

tion of using clamps which are permanently mounted to the press ram. In other words, they are "no-travel" clamps. With these clamps, tight tolerances are required. The subplate die set must extend out to the edge of the ram and bolster to use the clamp. Many times, due to clearance problems on top of the ram, special pockets have to be machined to provide room for the mounting of the clamp.

The most widely used of the no-travel clamps is the swing clamp (see **Figure 37**), which mounts onto the press slide or bottom of the press bed. These clamps are hydraulically or electrically activated to mechanically lock and unlock the clamp. Hydraulically-powered clamps require tighter tolerances of

+/- .008 inch to +/-.020 inch, depending on the type of design selected. The electrically-activated clamps can provide a clamping tolerance up to 1/4 inch. As shown in Figure 37, the clamp swings into position through a slot cut out of the die shoe or subplate. The clamp features automatic control of the swing action and monitoring of the clamping force.

The advantage of these clamps is the mechanically locking feature. Once activated by hydraulics or electrically, the clamp cannot be released until it is again activated. Therefore, once clamped, if an hydraulic or electric failure occurred, the clamp would remain clamped until the power source was again in operation

The disadvantage of these clamps is that they are very expensive. They can cost $2,500 to $3,000 per clamp, depending on the model selected plus the control package and hardware.

Another type of no-travel clamp is the clamping bar (see **Figure 38**). This type of clamp is permanently mounted to the faces of the bolster and ram. Clamping bar cylinders then clamp down on the backplate. This system requires a standard die configuration and a minimum of a 1-inch clamping surface along the backplates on two opposite sides of each tool.[4]

Selecting the Control System. The most widely used method is to use redundant control systems which require two controls. Both the top and bottom die shoes are controlled separately with redundancy and feedback. Two groups of clamps on two separate hydraulic lines hold each shoe. Holding pressure is continually monitored by pressure-sensitive microswitches. If pressure in any line drops below a preset pressure, the press will shut down.

---

[4]Enerpac Production Automation

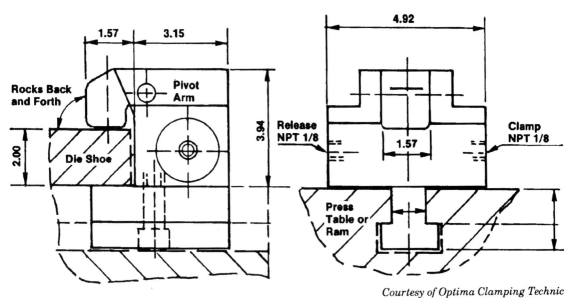

Courtesy of Optima Clamping Technic

Figure 36: Knuckle-type (pivot) clamp

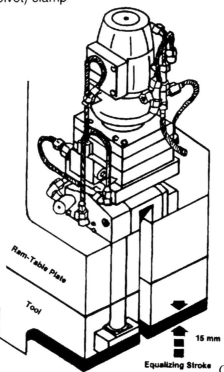

Figure 37: Swing-type clamp

Courtesy of Optima Clamping Technic

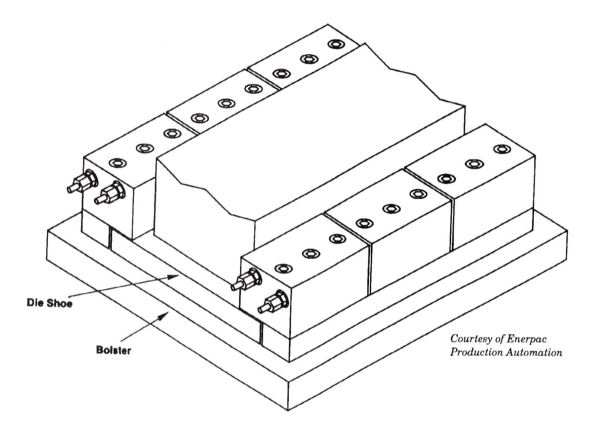

Die Shoe

Bolster

*Courtesy of Enerpac
Production Automation*

Figure 38: Clamping bar

Another method involves each clamp having its own sensing and monitoring device. Each is controlled separately with hydraulics. In this way, if one clamp fails, the others will still maintain pressure (see **Figure 39**). This method requires additional hard piping for installation and is more expensive, but it provides added safety.

The aforementioned method and equipment changes are some of the improvements available for reducing job change. You must continue to investigate and install method and hardware changes. Where you stop is dependent upon the goals your company has set based on manpower and monies allocated for the project.

44

Figure 39: Hydraulic pumping system

Selecting Your Die Handling System

5

Questions You Need to Ask

When selecting a die handling system, there is certain information that you should know before going out for quotes. This information will shorten the lead time for obtaining the quote and aid the engineer and his setup team in developing an equipment specification.

The following questions should be answered. The information should be available from your company.

- What is the goal for die exchange time?
- How many changeovers are to be performed per day with the unit?
- What type of method is presently being used for locating die in press?
- Is the die exchange to be performed by one man?
- Is the die handling system to be quoted as a turnkey?
- Is a floor plan available which shows all aisle dimensions of the press area, rack area, or transportation area where the unit should maneuver?
- Are the minimum and maximum sizes of dies known, such as length, width, height, and weight?
- Is the height from the top of the bolster or rack to the floor known?
- Is the distance that the dies are to be pushed into the press known?
- Is a continual push into the press required?
- What type of engagement or latching to the dies is required?
- How can we lock to the press during die exchange?
- Are all the dies to be subplated?
- Are there going to be die rollers in the press bolster to aid in the pushing and pulling of dies?
- Is there a preferred direction of travel for die insertion and removal? Right to left, or front to back?
- Is the unit to service multiple presses?
- What is the condition of the floor where the cart is to operate? Do you have a floor specification?

Equipment Alternatives

There are many different types of die handling systems from which to choose. The choice depends on die weights and desired die exchange time. The following is a summary of several different types used on both small (75 to 250 tons) and large (300 to 500 ton) presses. The material presented is not intended to be all-inclusive, but to provide the reader a basic understanding of die carts and the advantages and disadvantages they offer in reducing job change time.

Small Presses. For the small press group (75 to 250 tons), the simplest system using the existing fork truck is to purchase several bolster extensions (see **Figure 40**), which are bolted both to the floor and to the front of the press bolster. Bolster extensions

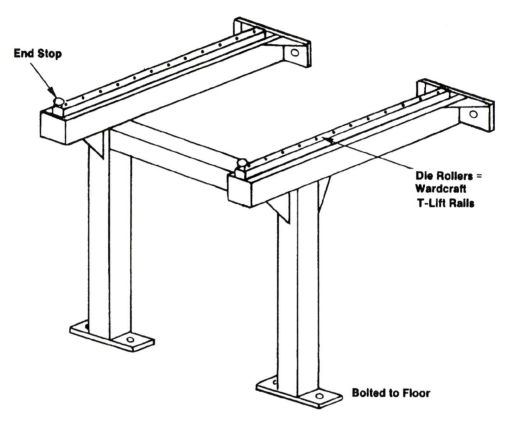

End Stop

**Die Rollers =
Wardcraft
T-Lift Rails**

Bolted to Floor

Figure 40: Bolster extensions (fixed locations)

can also be removable single or double swivel to allow the bolster extensions to be folded up and out of the way following the die exchange. In order to use this type of die exchange system, die rollers (air or hydraulic) must be installed in the press bolster, with prestage die racks provided nearby to allow the fork truck driver to aside the old die, obtain the new die, and return to the press in minimum time. The advantages of this system are:

- Low cost.
- Easy to install.

- Short lead time.
- Uses existing equipment for the die exchange.
- Uses rollers in the press bed for die positioning.

The disadvantages of the system are:

- Potential delays waiting for the fork truck driver.
- In most cases, two people are needed to make the die exchange. The fork truck driver asides the old die and gets the new die,

48

while the operator pushes and asides the dies on and off the bolster and positions the bolster extensions, if required.

• Dies cannot be prestaged at the rear of the press prior to start.

• Die exchange time is high because the old dies must be asided before the next die can be brought to the press. It is recommended to prestage the tools at a minimum distance from the press to reduce fork truck travel distances during the exchange process.

Another type of commonly-used, very simply-designed equipment is small ball roller tables or die carts (see **Figure 41**). The die carts include the cart/rotating table and the two-story quick die change cart. The roller transfer ball tables include the carrousel, two-station, and single-station styles. Two-station die carts are designed to unload the die and put in a new die without leaving the press. The advantages of this style are speed, maneuverability, and multiple use, but cost can be a disadvantage.

The carrousel style of roller transfer ball tables is a low-cost option. It can prestage a large quantity of dies at the press, and the operator can perform his own die exchange without outside interference from another person or equipment. However, this style takes up floor space and requires good scheduling practices to ensure the next die to run matches

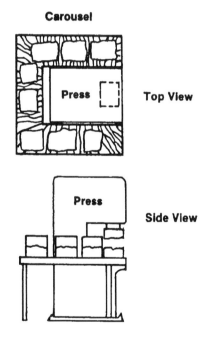

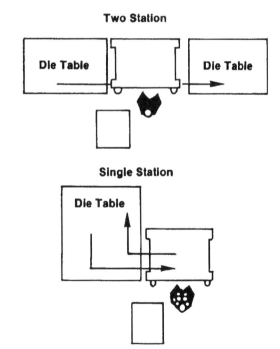

Courtesy of American Lifts

Figure 41: Roller ball tables

the material delivered to the press. If floor space or die flow dictates that a smaller table should be used, you can use a single table at only one side of the press or two small single tables (which hold one die only) located at each side of the press. The disadvantage of smaller tables is fewer dies stored at point of use.

The portable ball transfer-style cart (see **Figure 42**) has the advantages of low cost, compact size, and short lead time to build. Its disadvantage is that, with it, dies weighing only up to 1,000 pounds per side can be manually pushed.

By using these types of equipment for small presses, you can eliminate the use of a fork truck for die exchange. As **Figure 43** shows, replacing the use of the fork truck (old method) with die carts and fixed tables (new method) for die exchange will result in a significant reduction in time and be a lower cost option.

Large Presses. For the large press group (300 to 500 tons), you have the option of noncaptive or captive systems.

<u>Noncaptive Systems</u> service individual presses and transport the dies to and from die storage, the tool room, and the press. The most common are the fork truck, and flat bed or side-loader die trucks. The fork truck is widely used for loads up to 10,000 pounds.

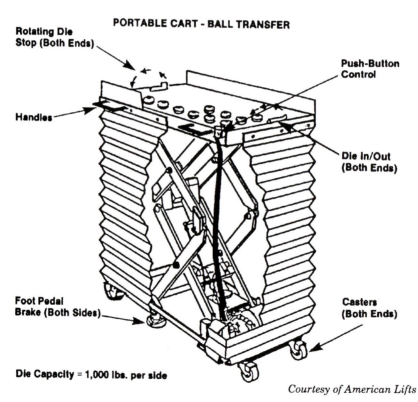

PORTABLE CART - BALL TRANSFER

Rotating Die Stop (Both Ends)

Push-Button Control

Handles

Die In/Out (Both Ends)

Foot Pedal Brake (Both Sides)

Casters (Both Ends)

Die Capacity = 1,000 lbs. per side

Courtesy of American Lifts

Figure 42: Portable cart—ball transfer

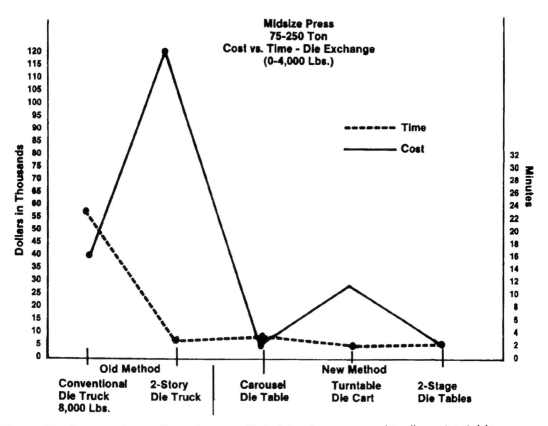

Figure 43: Cost vs. time—die exchange with fork truck as opposed to die cart or table

Once the die weight and size make the fork truck obsolete, a flat bed die truck is used. Die trucks can handle a wide variety of weights and can lift dies approximately 12 feet in the air for maximum die storage space. The main drawback to these vehicles is the actual die exchange. This equipment is large and difficult to maneuver in tight spaces. The result is frequent damage at the press and prestage die rack areas.

Most of the die trucks in use in U.S plants have an hydraulic push/pull mechanism with no means to automatically attach to the die. Therefore, the operator must get off the truck and wrap chains around the die to pull the die out of the press or rack. To aid die positioning, many people use keyways in the center of the press to align the die during the push/pull sequence.

An exception to the rule is the large bed die truck with its own die latching system (see **Figure 44**). The major advantage of this equipment is that the truck can both load and unload the die in the press and die storage and take the die to the tool repair area.

In today's environment of quick changing dies, many companies are splitting the die handling functions; the die truck services the

51

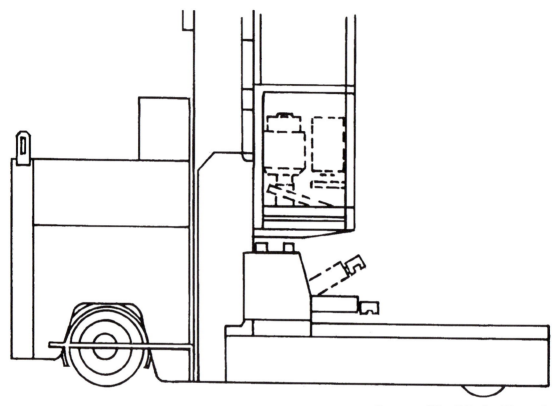

Figure 44: Flatbed die truck with automatic die attachment

Courtesy of Elwell-Parker Electric Co.

prestage die rack area and transports the dies to and from die storage and maintenance, while the die carts are purchased to perform the actual die exchange. Therefore, these carts become captive systems.

In summary, die trucks are advantageous because they have multiple uses. They can transport dies to and from die storage and in and out of the press. They can also store dies approximately 12 feet in the air. The disadvantages are that two people are required for the actual die exchange. Also, space for maneuvering is limited, because often, while one press is being changed over, the press next to it is shut down to allow the die truck to get between the presses. In addition, the average cost today to purchase a 50,000-ton capacity die truck is around $200,000, depending on options selected, and lead time is approximately one year for building.

Captive Systems. The term "captive systems" refers to die carts. The main purpose of the die carts is to exchange the dies in the presses and at the prestage die area.

Die carts can be air, wheel, or rail design, powered by air, hydraulics, or electronics. The die carts are self-contained, battery, or air-powered either from an overhead festoon or in the floor. They can have height adjustment varying from 12 up to 50 inches. Die carts can be compact and low-profile to enable the cart to load or unload dies off of the press bolster only 8 inches off the ground. For positioning at the press, infrared beams, lasers, or shot pins are commonly used. Most carts have their own push/pull mechanism and automatic die attachment features.

For lifting a small die, the scissors lift is widely used (see **Figure 45**). A common method for lifting large dies are screw jacks (see **Figure 46**).

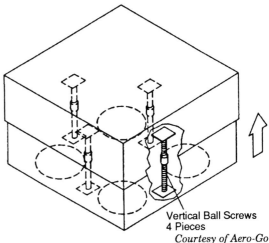

Vertical Ball Screws
4 Pieces
Courtesy of Aero-Go

Figure 46: Height adjustment with ball screws

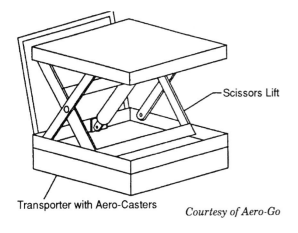

Scissors Lift

Transporter with Aero-Casters

Courtesy of Aero-Go

Figure 45: Height adjustment with scissors lift

* Air Die Carts. For comparison, several different types of die carts are here described. Again, this is not an all-inclusive list of equipment that may be available in the marketplace.

The single-station air die cart (see **Figure 47**) is driven into a pair of symmetrical wings located at the base of the press. These wings precisely align the cart so that the

centerline of the transporter lines up directly with the centerline of the press. This arrangement ensures die alignment each time. Next, the air bearings are deflated and the cart lowers to the floor. Two latching mechanisms engage the wings during deflation, physically locking the cart to the press and preventing any movement during the push/pull cycle.

The two-station air die cart (see **Figure 48**) was used by the author at a customer's company. The cart's capacity was 56,000 pounds, or 28,000 pounds per side. It had a fully automatic push/pull and die attachment and a reach of 66 inches. It also featured a fully synchronized dual drive system. The cart size was 104 inches, with a height of 49 inches.

The actual time to exchange dies with the cart in this installation was 100 minutes with one operator. The cycle is shown in **Figure 49**. Internal time (Items 1-7) is the actual die exchange at the press. Complete cycle time includes loading the new die at the

Figure 47: Single-station air die cart

prestage rack, exchanging the old die with the new die, unloading the old die at the prestage die rack, and obtaining the next new die.

Catch/pull lugs were bolted to the face of the die on both sides. V-notch locators are added to the die set for positioning the die inside of the press bolster. For safety, a reflector was mounted on both the prestage die racks and at the press. With this, a signal could be projected from the die cart to the reflector, then received back at the die cart. If a signal would be received, the operator would

Figure 48: Two-station air rotating die cart

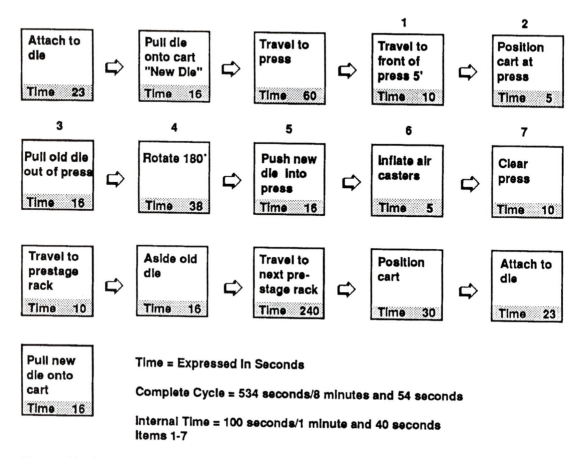

Attach to die Time 23	⇨	Pull die onto cart "New Die" Time 16	⇨	Travel to press Time 60	⇨	Travel to front of press 5' Time 10 (1)	⇨	Position cart at press Time 5 (2)

1 Travel to front of press 5' **Time 10**
2 Position cart at press **Time 5**

3 Pull old die out of press **Time 16** ⇨ **4** Rotate 180° **Time 38** ⇨ **5** Push new die into press **Time 16** ⇨ **6** Inflate air casters **Time 5** ⇨ **7** Clear press **Time 10**

Travel to prestage rack **Time 10** ⇨ Aside old die **Time 16** ⇨ Travel to next pre-stage rack **Time 240** ⇨ Position cart **Time 30** ⇨ Attach to die **Time 23**

Pull new die onto cart **Time 16**

Time = Expressed In Seconds

Complete Cycle = 534 seconds/8 minutes and 54 seconds

Internal Time = 100 seconds/1 minute and 40 seconds
Items 1–7

Figure 49: Sequence of operation—turntable die cart

be able to operate the push/pull mechanism and retrieve or push off the die set.

The distance that the signal could travel and be recognized by the controls on the die cart was 12 inches. If the cart was further than 12 inches away from the press or die rack, the push/pull mechanism would not function. This would prevent the operator from accidentally pushing off the die set from the die cart onto the floor before reaching the press bed or die rack.

The advantages of the air cart are:

• Maneuverability – It can maneuver in very tight corners, allowing the cart to travel between presses and exchange dies at one press without shutting down the second press.

• Ease of operation – The operator can change direction with the push of a button on the air logic controls.

• Cost – It is easy to justify because

several presses can be serviced with one die cart.

• Multiple directions – The cart can travel in the XY axes or steer off on diagonal traffic patterns to allow the cart to steer around stock tubs or other equipment.

• Travel speed – The cart can travel from 40 to 80 FPM.

The main disadvantage of the air die cart is its flooring requirements. The floor must be free of pitted concrete and slope within 1/8 inch in 10 feet. If the floor is to be resurfaced, an option is to burn off approximately 1/8 inch of existing concrete and replace it with an epoxy floor. A wood block floor would have to be replaced with a steel or poured concrete surface.

Air die carts use a specialized material handling device called the air caster. The die carts use multiple air casters to lift the load to minimize drive force for transporting.

Figure 50 shows a cross section of a single Aero-Caster element. In the first step, when the air caster is at rest, the load is solidly supported on the landing pads. Arrows in the figure represent air flow. In the second step, air enters the flexible torus bag and plenum chamber. The torus bag inflates and seals against the floor. Finally, in step three, when air pressure in the plenum chamber exceeds the load weight, air escapes evenly under the torus bag. The load now floats on a thin film of compressed air.

There is a continuous flow of air creating a thin film of air 3/1,000 to 5/1,000 inch thick. On this cushion, the load can be conveyed, positioned, rotated, or transferred in any direction with a force of only 3 pounds per 1,000 pounds of load. For a level, sealed concrete floor, only 90 pounds of force are required to move 30,000 pounds.

The air caster is based upon the fundamental law of mechanics: force equals pressure times area. Since the contact area is relatively large for air casters as compared to wheels, floor loading for large die carts is minimized.

To give you an idea of the high capacity-to-size ratio, a 21-inch diameter air caster has

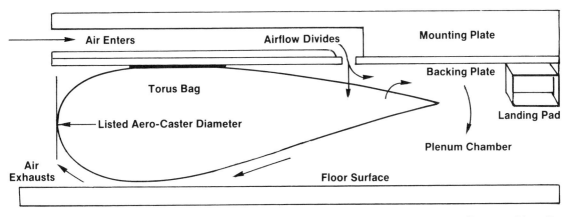

Courtesy of Aero-Go

Figure 50: Cross section of Aero-Caster element

a fixed 280 square inch area. When pressurized to 25 PSIG, it yields 7,000 pounds of capacity per bearing. Thus, a die cart with four each of 21-inch air casters has a total lift capacity of 28,000 pounds (weight of dies plus cart weight).

Typical air casters used in carts have the following ranges:

- Diameter = 15 inches to 48 inches
- Capacity = 14,000 to 160,000 pounds
- Air Consumption = 98 to 182 SCFM

* Wheel Die Cart. Due to the special floor requirements of the air die carts, a new die cart system has now been developed. The same technology for steering the air die cart has been applied to a wheel-type die cart. The new wheel die cart offers a multiple direction vehicle that is able to operate on wood block and poor concrete surface areas. The cart uses air technology with wheeled casters for stability to provide a multiple directional die cart that can operate on most floor surfaces (see **Figure 51**). It has synchronized steering, enabling the die cart to travel in a straight line or veer to the left or right. The system consists of two air steerable drive motors and four spindle caster wheels for stability.

* Rail Die Carts. One example of a rail die cart is shown in **Figure 52**. The two-station rail cart is automated, with a 60,000-

Figure 51: Dual-station wheel vehicle, air-powered (capacity = 24,000 lbs.)

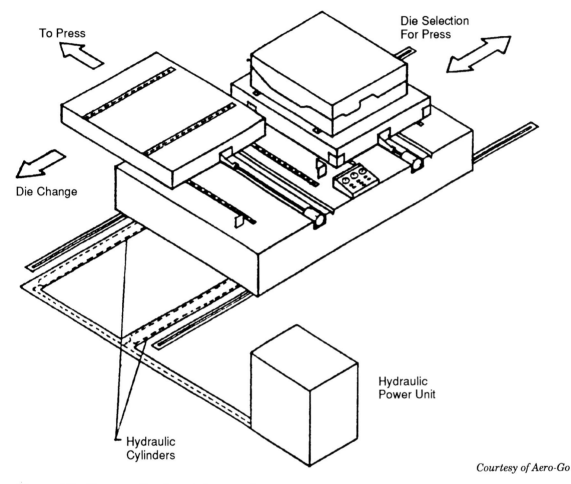

To Press

Die Selection
For Press

Die Change

Hydraulic
Power Unit

Hydraulic
Cylinders

Courtesy of Aero-Go

Figure 52: Express die change transporter

pound total capacity (30,000 pounds per side) to service one press. This concept is significantly different from previous examples, since the die and bolster are pulled from the side of the press instead of pulling just the die from the front. The advantage of exchanging dies from the side is to eliminate the requirement of moving conveyors and/or automation between presses.

The die exchange time is one minute for this system. The maximum bolster size for this cart is 96 inches by 54 inches, with a bolster height of 23 inches.

* **T-Tables**. Another approach to die change is the T-table. This concept uses hydraulic or air T-slot lifters in the press bolster, plus side guides or a keyway to control left to right location. As in the previous systems, dies are mounted to subplates so that all sizes of dies appear to be the same size to the die change system. A three-station powered roller conveyor table is mounted behind and parallel to the bed of the press (see **Figure 53**). Pivoted or fixed bolster extensions equipped with rollers are mounted to this table and pinned to the bed of the press when the die is about to be moved. This pivoting feature allows easy access to the press.

The camfollower rollers on the extensions provide support and side guiding for the die/subplate as it is being removed from the press. The hydraulic T-slot lifters are raised after the die is unclamped from the bolster. Heavier dies are rolled out using a powered push/pull module.

A new die is located on one end of the three-station powered conveyor. After the die is removed from the press, it is lowered onto the powered conveyor and both the old die and the new die are moved simultaneously one way to place the new die in the center of the conveyor and in line with the press. The new die is then rolled into the press to a fixed stop. The hydraulic T-slot lifters are lowered and the die is bolted or hydraulically clamped to the bolster.

For the lighter die installations, a manual system uses a two-station linear actuator. In this type of system, the die is pulled out of the press onto one linear actuator carriage equipped with nonpowered rollers. This carriage is pushed to one side and the second carriage with the new die is pushed into the center position. The new die is pushed into the press and clamped in final position.

The major disadvantage of the T-table system is that it takes up a fixed area behind the press. The advantages of the system are low costs and quick changes without use of fork lift trucks or cranes. In addition, this system does not affect either side or the front of the press and can be used for two presses back to back with the addition of another set of bolster extensions on the other side of the table.[5]

In summary, as shown in **Figure 54**, several different die cart options can result in different expenses of time and money. The figure shows a comparison among several different die cart options with regard to time saved versus cost of the equipment. Die exchange time can be significantly reduced by purchasing captive die cart systems. We are now reaching an age in manufacturing in which press downtime for die exchange must be minimized. Therefore, these types of die handling options must be investigated and compared to the conventional method of die handling using die trucks.

A Sample Selection Process

In the actual selection process of a specific die handling system for a particular plant, the engineer or project team must evaluate different equipment choices with certain project goals and layout constraints. For example, one of the companies for which the author consulted investigated several die handling options for servicing several straight-side coil feed presses. To reduce present die exchange from approximately 20 minutes to

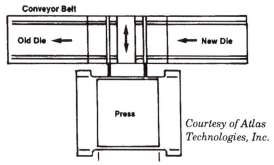

Courtesy of Atlas Technologies, Inc.

Figure 53: Power roller table shuttle system

[5]Atlas Technologies, Inc.

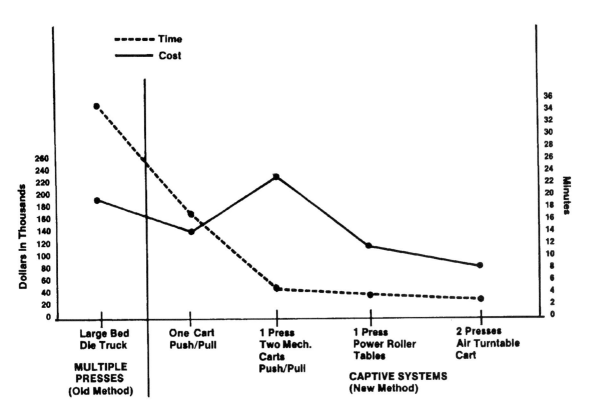

Figure 54: Cost vs. time—die exchange with captive systems as opposed to noncaptive systems for dies weighing approximately 30,000 lbs.

under five minutes, the following alternatives were investigated.

Alternative A was to use two-tier die storage racks serviced by die carts with lift height capabilities from 40 to 66 inches (see **Figure 55**). It involved six die carts, 54 dies stored, and 2,300 square feet for die storage. Due to the 26-inch lift requirement and the complexity of the die cart, this option was eliminated early for consideration.

Alternative B was a two-station (side by side) rail die cart with push/pull from one side of the press only (see **Figure 56**). It involved

three die carts and 15 stored dies. There was 480 square feet for storing the dies. This layout reduced congestion around the presses and required less storage space, but the length of the die cart (14 feet, 3 inches) interfered with the operator station and the coil change operation. For this reason, Alternative B was rejected by the setup team.

Alternative C involved one air/rail die cart with turntable, servicing all three presses, and one new die truck to load and unload dies from a three-tier rack system (see **Figure 57**). The cart would be used to just exchange dies

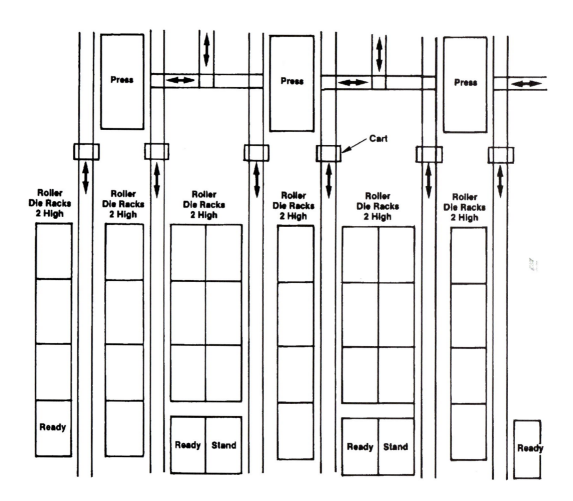

Figure 55: Alternative A

and load/unload dies at the three designated prestage die racks. A die truck would transport dies to and from the tool room, load and unload dies in die storage areas, and prestage dies for the die carts. Seventy-five dies could be stored, and 3,000 square feet were used for storing the dies.

The consensus of the group was that this layout had some merit. It provided maximum die storage and a backup system for die carts if the die cart was out of commission. It also opened up space for storing stock tubs. Only one die cart would be required, which would simplify the scheduling of manpower during the die exchange. One major drawback could occur if two presses had to be changed over at the same time, but the group considered this a minor problem, since all jobs to run for that

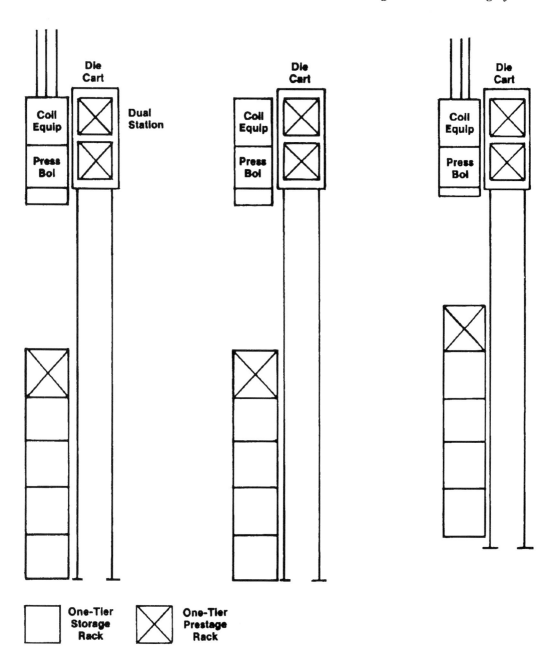

Figure 56: Alternative B

63

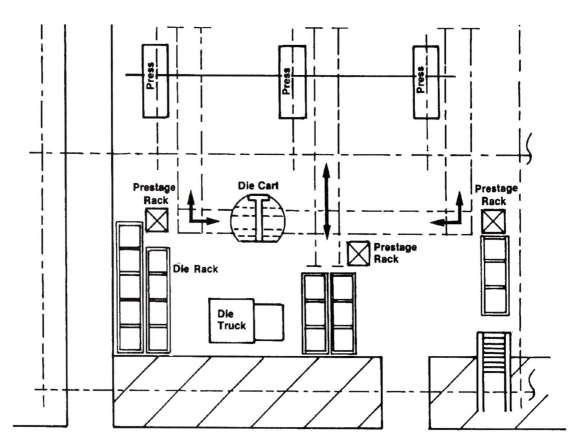

Figure 57: Alternative C

day would be scheduled ahead of time.

A fourth alternative was proposed that would involve the design, fabrication, and delivery of a complete quick die change system in accordance with Alternative C, except that an air cart would replace the rail cart. This would eliminate the use of rails in the floor.

The Decision. To aid in the team's decision process, trips were made to see both rail and air die carts in use. After submitting the quotation, a followup visit was made to review

the quotation and conduct an onsite decision analysis comparing the various die handling alternatives. The people present at this visit were the project coordinator, the production foreman, setup people, and the builder of the die carts.

In comparing the alternatives, the company identified several benefits it wanted from the handling system, and weighted them in order of importance (10 = highest, 1 = lowest). The results were:

• Minimized die exchange time 10

- Minimized disruption at the
  press   9
- Minimized disruption at the
  staging area for loading stock
  tubs   9
- Simplified manpower scheduling
  for press operation   8
- Minimized installation costs and
  time   7
- Minimized cost   6
- Compatible backup system   6
- Storage of all dies at the press   6
- Maximized floor space for tub
  storage   5

After comparing the various alternatives, a single die cart was selected. Due to steering requirements for maneuvering around stock containers and scrap conveyors, an air die cart was selected over a rail die cart to minimize disruption at the press during the job change.

Reasons for the Choice. The main reason for the company's choice of the air cart over the rail was the ability of the cart to maneuver around prestage storage containers and portable scrap conveyors. Due to the congestion around the presses, the company decided that the rail cart was not the answer.

In contrast, another company desired one die cart to travel in a fixed path to and from the prestage die rack to the press. The only use intended for this die cart was to exchange dies in the press and transport dies to and from the prestage die rack. In this case, a rail die cart was selected.

Many factors must be weighed while you investigate the various die handling alternatives. One particular die cart design will not meet every company's needs. The task of the engineering team in charge of the project is to gather information about the various die designs available in the market. They must establish certain musts and wants to aid the selection process. As shown in Figure 54, when comparing certain die cart designs, the time saved and money spent to meet desired goals will determine the type of die cart selected.

Case Studies

6

Gehl Corporation Case Study – Small Press Dies

The following case study involves the implementation of quick die change at Gehl Corporation, West Bend, Wisconsin.

In July, 1978, top management at Gehl realized that they needed to change how they manufactured stampings in their press area. Lot sizes were getting smaller, which resulted in more daily setups. Business was booming, so presses were over capacity. This resulted in long (50-hour) work weeks for all three shifts.

To determine a direction to take, two employees were sent to attend a two-day seminar on quick die change. These employees were the plant superintendent and the supervisor of process and tool engineering. Following the seminar and approval from top management, a steering committee was formed to head up the company's quick die change effort. Gehl's steering committee held periodic meetings with the press room hourly employees.

As a result of these meetings, the steering committee put together a proposal for reworking two presses. These two presses were singled out as test cases. The presses would be retrofitted with quick die change and results in job change time would be computed. Following an evaluation, the company would determine if the remaining presses would be retrofitted in the same way.

In early September, 1987, Gehl Corporation commissioned a three-week feasibility study which would take into account the total plant requirements for die handling and material flow within the plant. After a review of the study's findings by top management, approval was given to proceed with the project. A project schedule was developed, and actual implementation of the retrofit began in early December, 1987. The purchase and installation of the quick die change equipment was accomplished in six months. Gehl's responsibility was to purchase equipment to prestage the material which was still under investigation at the plant.

The hardware and equipment installation resulted in a reduction in job change time from 90 minutes to 14 minutes on the 150-ton OBI press, and a reduction in job change time from 90 minutes to 18 minutes on the 200-ton straight-side press.

Parameters

On the 150-ton OBI press, the maximum die size was 44 inches by 24 inches, while minimum die size was 12 inches by 6 inches. Maximum die weight was 1,200 pounds. It included 50 tools and had a bolster size of 50 inches right to left and 33 inches front to back. On the 200-ton straight-side press, the maximum die size was 48 inches by 36 inches. The minimum die size was 15 inches by 12 inches, and the maximum die weight was 2,000 pounds. It had 50 tools and its bolster size was 54 inches right to left and 48 inches front to back.

Notes were made that the bolsters were not JIC, and provisions needed to be made by Gehl for subplating dies and standardizing shut heights. Changeover time referred to part-in, part-out. The cushion pin hole pattern in the existing bolsters remained the same.

Plan of Action

The first step taken was to formulate a plan of action together with the Gehl steering committee (see **Figure 58**). This project

schedule addressed the method and equipment changes to be investigated to reduce job change on one 200-ton straight-side press and one 150-ton OBI press.

This plan of action was two-fold. In the short term, the company wanted to investigate press modifications and hardware purchases to retrofit the existing 150-ton press and 200-ton press. This included ram and bolster revisions. In the long term, the company wanted to investigate die handling equipment for both presses. The equipment would be purchased and tested. If successful, this equipment would be used on additional

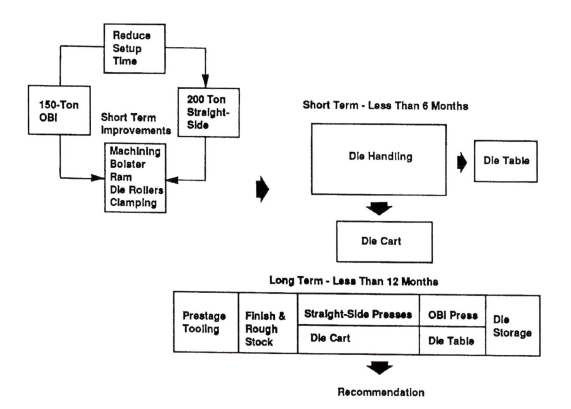

Figure 58: Gehl case study—plan of action

presses for both the plant in Wisconsin and a plant in South Dakota.

To identify costs and potential savings with lead times, the author conducted a three-week engineering study. That study resulted in the following recommendations:

- All dies should have their own individual storage location.
- An existing fork truck will be used to transport tooling to and from the prestage die rack to storage and die repair.
- A new die handling system will be purchased for die exchange.
- All dies will be mounted on subplates. Three sizes of subplates will be used throughout the company for present and new die sets.
- Cushion pins will now be stored with each die set.
- Tooling to produce high user parts will be stored close to the point of use.
- The following information will be labeled on all press dies:
  - shut height
  - part number
  - weight
  - front, rear of die set
  - cushion pin length
- All press tooling will be prestaged at the press. The existing rack will be revised with ball rollers. The die will be located the same in the prestage rack as in the press, and locating pins will be used to align the die in the rack.
- Mechanical die clamps will be used for the 200-ton press, while a manual die clamp (two turns) will be used for the 150-ton press.
- Ball transfer tables are recommended for the 150-ton press, and an air die cart (two-station) is recommended for the 200-ton press.
- The high users will be subplated first.

Die Standardization

In reviewing the dies used in the 200-ton press, statistics were gathered about the number of times the die is set up, the number of dies, the run hours, and the setup hours (see **Figure 59**)

If the company would rework only the dies that were scheduled over five times, the following expenses would occur and 71 percent of run time and 69 percent of setup time would be covered.

The expenses for subplating would be two plates per die at $200 each, and four hours rework per die at $25.00 each or $100. So, $400 (plates) + $100 (labor) = $23,000 for the rework of this category of dies on the 200-ton press.

Suggestions for subplating the dies were to subplate:

- All tools.
- High users (run more than 10 times in one year), running other tooling on the weekend.
- High users, running them together with low users which are not subplated.
- High users, mounting low user tooling onto subplates before each production run and tearing down after each production run.

Due to the cost for subplates, the recommendation was to purchase several subplates and assemble dies to the subplates in the tool room before each run. In all high production jobs, all dies would be permanently subplated immediately.

To develop lead times for project implementation, a project schedule in the form of a critical path chart was developed (see **Figure 60**). This project schedule explains the work content required to implement quick die

# of Times Die Setup	# of Dies	Run Hrs.	Setup Hrs.
10 and Over	29	1,438.0	2,013.3
9	2	26.9	20.4
8	2	11.2	14.4
7	4	38.7	35.6
6	9	76.7	87.8
Sub Total	46	1,591.5	2,171.5
5 and Under	114	644.9	960.8
Total	160	2,236.4	3,132.3

Figure 59: Statistics for die standardization subplates

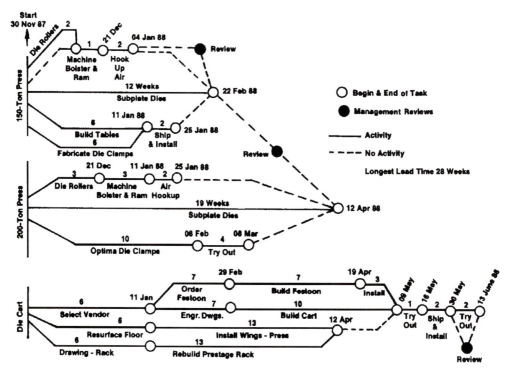

Figure 60: Gehl case study—project schedule in critical path chart form

change on the 150- and 200-ton presses. The work was divided into three categories:

• Quick change hardware, methods, and improvements for the 150-ton press.
• Quick change hardware, methods, and improvements for the 200-ton press.
• The purchase of one die cart to service the straight-side press group.

All tasks were clearly defined with the estimated target dates. The longest lead item (28 weeks) was the purchase of the die cart.

To address method and equipment changes, revise old methods on the 150-ton press, and reduce job change time from 90 minutes with two people to under 15 minutes with one person, the following improvements were implemented:

• Provided a new ram adapter plate with 3/4-inch T-slots
• Provided new bolster with 3/4-inch T-slots and installed new air bag die roller system, allowing the die to travel two different directions on the bolster
• Die positioning – added two locating pins in the bolster and V-notch locators were machined in all bottom subplates.

150-Ton Press

With the old method on the 150-ton press, (see **Figure 61**) die exchange time started at 15 minutes with two people (press operator and fork truck driver) and clamp/unclamp time was 25 minutes. With the new method, die exchange was substantially reduced to 1.5 minutes, and clamp/unclamp

Figure 61: 150-ton press—old method

time was reduced to a mere three minutes (see **Figure 62 and 63**). To achieve these reduced times, die positioning was facilitated in the press. To do this, a method of using two locating pins in the bolster was selected. The die plates would have V-notch cutouts on which to locate the subplate. **Figure 64** shows this method. The edges may be flame cut, except for zones A & B, which must have a 125 finish. All sharp edges must be broken.

To standardize all tooling for both the OBI and straight-side presses, three plate sizes were selected for the plant. The locations of the V-notches in the plates were identical, although the width and length of the three plate sizes could vary.

To aid die positioning in the press, two-directional air bag die rollers were used. One set of the two rollers would raise to move the die right to left. To move the die front to back and right to left, the roller section would be lowered, and the other set of rollers (12 inches long) would be raised to aid in the pushing and pulling (see **Figure 65**). On the air bag die rollers, the valve for raising and lowering the die rollers was located below the operator's palm buttons for easy access.

Die Clamping Recommendations. The general consensus regarding the die clamping was that by having different clamping systems on the two presses, a com-

Figure 62: 150-ton press—new method

**Die Table
Transfer**

**Ball Transfer
Entrance Table**

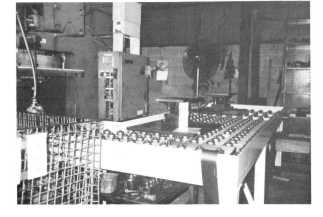

**Prestaging Die
while Press
is Running**

Figure 63: 150-ton press—specifics of new method

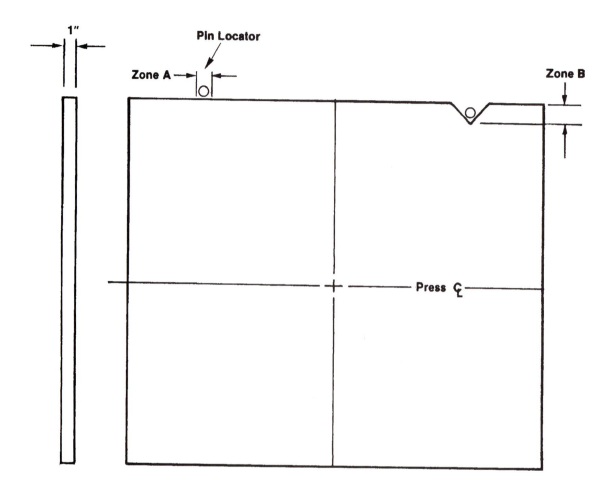

Figure 64: Die positioning via two locating pins in the bolster

parison could be made between the pros and cons, and this data would be used to determine what would be purchased on the next machines to be retrofitted.

The recommended clamps for the 150-ton OBI press were the T-bolt design mechanical clamps (see **Figure 66**). Eight mechanical T-bolt die clamps would be used (four on top, four on bottom). Three maximum turns of a box head wrench were needed for tightening or untightening the clamp to the die shoe. Hydraulic clamping was put on hold, because the money could be used to pay for a die handling system for the 200-ton press.

Die Handling Alternatives. The alternatives given to Gehl for die handling on the 150-ton press were either a carrousel on

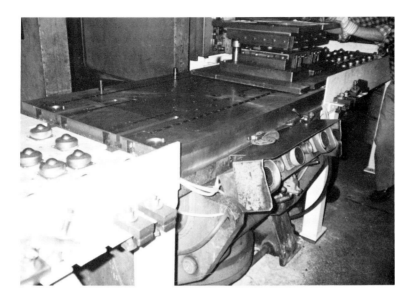

Figure 65: Sliding the die over rollers in the bolster

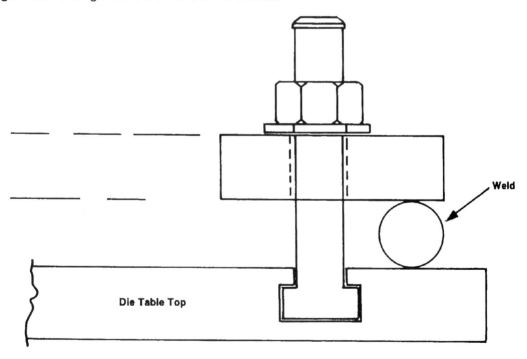

Weld

Die Table Top

Figure 66: 150-ton OBI press clamp recommendation—T-bolt mechanical

all sides of the press, or a partial carrousel, with the back of the press left open for die loading and retrieval.

After a review of the alternatives, the second option was selected. One reason for the selection was that there was a concern about how long it would take to develop a scheduling system to support this press. The consensus was that the dies would have to be delivered in a systematic ordering system to ensure die positioning. A second reason for the choice was the cost. A partial carrousel costs approximately 20 percent less than a full carrousel. Finally, with the first option, dies would be loaded and unloaded behind the press, away from the main traffic aisle. This made it difficult for the fork truck driver to maneuver due to tight space constraints behind the press.

200-Ton Press

Die Clamping Recommendations. To address method and equipment changes and revise the old method on the 200-ton press (see **Figure 67**), and to reduce job change time from 120 minutes with two people, the following improvements were implemented (see **Figure 68**):

- Provided new bolster with 1-inch T-slots and installed air bag die rollers (see **Figure 69**)
- Provided portable machining services to machine 1-inch T-slots in the press ram
- Added two pin locators for die positioning. It is identical to the method used in the 150-ton press for locating
- Die clamping—mechanical die clamps

Figure 67: 200-ton press—old method

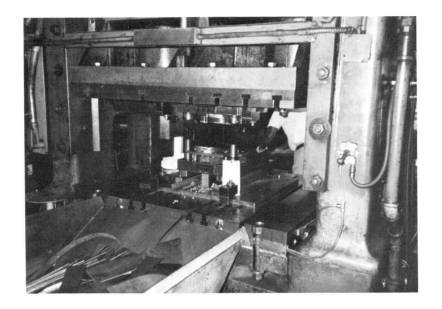

Figure 68: 200-ton press—new method

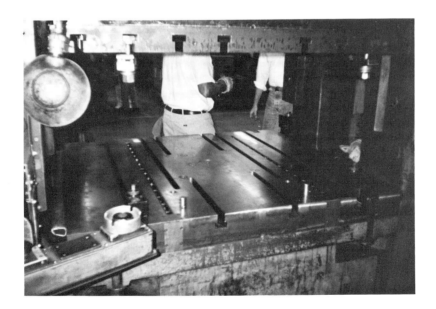

Figure 69: 200-ton press—added 1-inch T-slots and air bag die rollers

The die clamp recommended for the 200-ton press was the Optima MEE mechanical die clamp (see **Figure 70**). The clamp slides into the existing T-slot until the clamp sits on the die shoe. It is then hand tightened so that the clamping screw makes solid contact with the die shoe. With a hex head wrench (11/16 inches or 17 millimeters), the power nut is turned 180 degrees until it reaches its stop and the arrow is pointing toward the green dot. To unclamp, the procedure is reversed.

Figure 71 shows two Optima die clamps pushed back after unclamping the upper die shoe. Since the die exchange occurs at the front of the press, there is no need to manually aside the die clamps. Instead, they can remain inside the T-slot of the press.

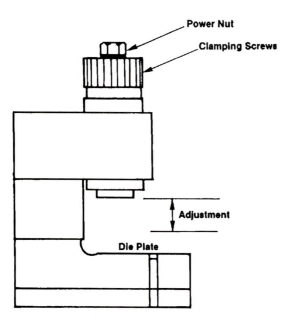

Courtesy of Optima Clamping Technic

Figure 70: Optima MEE mechanical die clamp

Die Handling Alternatives. Next, a decision had to be made about a die handling system. Team members were responsible for the development of the design and machine specification for the proposed die cart. To select the die cart system, a decision analysis was conducted with the following team members present:

- Press operators (5)
- Production foreman
- Process and tool engineer
- Process and tool supervisor
- Plant engineer

The team decided that the die handling system must service three straight-side presses and be compatible with subplated die sets. In addition, the operator must be able to push and pull 2,000 pounds with the cart, or two people must be able to push or pull 4,000 pounds.

Along with these necessities, certain objectives were identified by the team members for the handling system. It should minimize overall cost, maintenance costs, installation costs, and die exchange time (the team's goal was under three minutes). The system should maximize flexibility, so that the operator of a press could perform his own die exchange without the need of a fork truck. One die cart should service multiple presses and minimize congestion around those presses. There should be no die exchange in the main aisles, and bar stock should be run from both sides of the press.

Die handling equipment alternatives included:

- Single die cart - battery-powered
- Two-story die truck
- Two individual die carts - rail travel
- Two-station air die cart

Figure 71: Two Optima die clamps after unclamping upper die shoe

The team made its selection based on how the die handling alternatives met its objectives.

Single Die Cart. One of the options was a single die cart that was battery-powered. The cart had a capacity of 4,200 pounds, measuring 54 inches right to left, and 44 inches front to back. Its height adjustment was from 35 inches to 45 inches. The die rollers were on top and steering was controlled by a hand-held swivel. Die exchange time on such a cart was 12 minutes. Although it had advantages in cost and height adjustment, and floor resurfacing was not required for its use, its disadvantages included more time to dock at press, the exchange time, and the recharging of the battery.

Two-Story Die Truck. Another of the options for die handling was a battery-powered two-story die truck. Its maximum weight for both levels was 10,000 pounds. The die size measured 54 inches right to left and 44 inches front to back. Height adjustment was from 12 inches to 45 inches. The die rollers were on top and steering was swivel style. Die exchange time with the two-story die truck was two minutes. The short exchange time and the height adjustment were its advantages, as well as the fact that floor resurfacing was not required. However, more time required to dock at press and cost were disadvantages, as was the recharging of the battery.

One Two-Station or Two Individual Die Carts – Rail Travel. This option was vetoed early by the study team because of fixed travel. Additionally, it would block the main traffic aisle during the die exchange.

Two-Station Air Die Cart. The die handling system finally chosen for Gehl was the two-station air die cart (see **Figure 72**).

Figure 72: Two-station air die cart

With a capacity of 6,000 pounds, it measured 48 inches right to left and 60 inches front to back. The height adjustment was 35 inches to 45 inches. It had T-lift die rollers and its steering was controlled by a 90-degree drive wheel.

The die exchange with this cart was just 1.5 minutes. Cart height could be adjusted for different press bolster heights and centering positioning was accomplished via the use of guide wings installed at the base of the press. With this cart, the operator could perform a job change by himself. Finally, it allowed minimum delay time during the job change because the die could be prestaged on the cart.

A typical die change sequence involves the following steps:

1. A die transporter with a new die aligns the empty station (on transporter) with the press and docks.

2. The old die is moved onto the die transporter.

3. The die transporter undocks, travels away from the press, and is rotated 180 degrees by the operator. The die transporter again docks with the press, and the new die is automatically aligned with the press.

4. The new die is moved onto the press bolster.

5. The die transporter with the old die undocks from the press.

Prestage Recommendations. Gehl's prestage rack system for large presses is shown in **Figure 73**. This rack design permits loading and unloading in the front via a die cart and in the rear via a fork truck. The suggested revisions for this rack were to

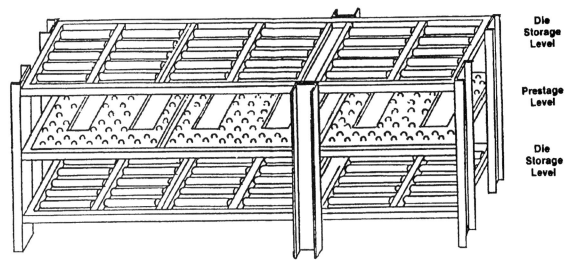

Die
Storage
Level

Prestage
Level

Die
Storage
Level

Figure 73: Gehl's prestage rack system

shorten the existing rack and remove the rollers from the center section of the die rack and replace them with a ball roller system.

It was Gehl's responsibility to remove the roller sections from the center shelf and add supports on both sides of the fork openings (a support measured 3 inches by 3 inches by 48 inches). Three plates were to be installed with ball rollers, a plate size being 1/2 inch by 54 inches by 48 inches. The company also had to cut an opening in 3-inch angle beam for fork clearance, making a total of six cutouts. The consultant's responsibility was to provide three plates with ball rollers mounted to them, with the plate size the same as above.

At the front of the rack, dies are loaded and unloaded manually using the air die cart. At the rear of the rack, dies are loaded and unloaded using a fork truck.

Prestage Die Table. Gehl's prestage die

[6]STAMPING Quarterly®

table for its presses weighing 2,500 pounds or less was a roller ball style (see **Figure 74**). The die prestage rack was serviced by a conventional fork truck. The fork truck driver would load and unload press dies on the middle shelf while the press operator ran production.

Prestage Die Change System. The prestage die change system consisted of the press operator walking approximately 20 feet to the die cart, loading the die onto the die chart, driving to the press and exchanging the old die with the new die, and returning the cart to the prestage rack and aside die. The total estimated time of this change was four minutes. To aid in the manual pushing and pulling, a disappearing air bag die roller was mounted to the top of the die cart (see **Figure 75**).

John Deere Case Study[6]

This case study involves John Deere, a manufacturer of lawn and garden equipment in Horicon, Wisconsin. The need for a quick

Figure 74: Roller ball prestage die table

Figure 75: Disappearing air bag die roller mounted to top of die cart

die change system at the press became apparent when the company subplated all of its 500-ton press tooling. A conventional fork truck had been used to pick up a typical 6,000-pound die and position it on the bed of one of the two 500-ton presses. Fork truck handling of the dies always presented the danger of a die slipping off the forks. It also required extensive maneuvering while aligning the die with the press bolster.

Multiple, single-die sets required multiple handlings until all the dies in the press were changed over. To speed up the process, the company developed a common die plate to mount the individual die sets. By subplating, the number of die sets requiring fork trucking for changeover was reduced from 107 to 61. To accomplish this reduction, new equipment had to be purchased because the die weights increased from 8,000 up to 30,000 pounds.

The following equipment was required in the press shop in a time frame that coincided with subplating the tooling:

• A 60,000-pound capacity conventional large bed die truck for transporting dies to and from die storage and positioning dies in the prestage die racks.
• A new die cart system capable of handling 30,000-pound die sets was required to minimize the time for exchanging the existing die with the new die during changeover.

Organizing the Project

A project manager was asked to develop a plan and organize a project team. To organize the project, a plan of action was developed by the project manager (see **Figure 76**). He then assembled representatives from various support departments to form a project team. The following team members were responsible for developing the design and machine specifications and selecting the vendor.

• Project manager, process and tool (1)
• Plant engineer (1)
• Crib supervisor (1)
• Industrial engineer (1)
• Production supervisor (1)
• Hourly - production (2)
• Hourly - maintenance (1)

The team's must/want list looked like this:

Musts:
• Compatible with all tools
• Maintain safety levels
• No building expansion

Wants:
• Not to exceed $200,000
• Minimize job change time
• Maximize flexibility
• Minimize maintenance repairs
• Maximize floor space
• Maximize quality levels
• Minimize lead time
• Minimize disruption in press area
• Maximize ROI (return on investment)
• Minimize die preparation

Once the concept was developed, the team used participative techniques and fact-finding trips to develop machine specifications. The die exchange sequence of unloading, loading, and attachment was to be done within five minutes.

Capacity requirements were developed. Maximum die weight was to be 30,000 pounds. Maximum die length was to be 120 inches, right to left, while maximum die width was to be 60 inches front to back. Maximum die shut

Plan Of Action

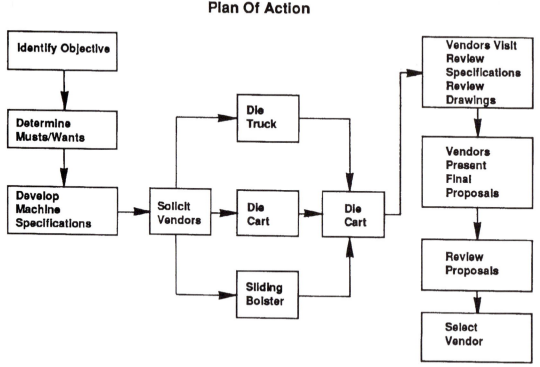

Figure 76: Deere case study—plan of action

height was to be 30 inches. The push/pull mechanism had to be able to push the die at least 15 inches inside of the press bolster. The system had to be compatible with all press dies that run on the 500-ton presses. It had to interface with existing prestage die racks. A minimum of a 3-inch height adjustment was required. Die rollers had to be used on the top surface of the die cart. The maximum turning radius was 13 feet. The system also had to maximize safety for die handling and transportation.

Fact-finding trips led to the conclusion that, to their knowledge, there was no equipment in the United States or overseas that would meet their specific requirements.

Therefore, the team decided to select a machine builder in the U.S. to design and build a one-of-a-kind express die change system to fit the specification.

The Alternatives

In the search for a vendor, the following die transportation alternatives were evaluated:

Conventional Die Trucks. The purchase of two die trucks was considered, but they would not meet the requirements for increased speed, safety, maneuverability, and minimizing die exchange time. Plus, the turning radius would have been prohibitive.

Retrofit Press with Sliding Bolsters. This would allow exchange of the die on the bolster outside the press. It had two bolster plates and two self-propelled transport carts. Its dimensions were 120 inches left to right and 60 inches front to back. Existing presses could be retrofitted with sliding bolsters, and the retrofitting would result in minimum die changeover time and allow the use of hydraulic clamping through the use of adaptor plates. However, this was the most expensive alternative. Production would be disrupted during installation, the press would have to be revised, and a long lead time would be involved. Overall, this option would be difficult to justify. Due to the cost of retrofitting and the disruption of production, this alternative was not recommended.

Mechanical Cart. Another alternative the team investigated was to purchase two rails-in-the-floor mechanical carts per press. One cart would pull the existing die out of the press. The second cart would simultaneously push in the new die. These types of die carts have proven to be a success in Japan.

Mechanical carts are a proven method of quick change that carry the advantages of minimum die changeover time and the ability to accurately locate the die in the press. Their cost, however, is a disadvantage. Also, dies must be revised, and two carts are required per press. As the sliding bolster option, this option was also difficult to justify. Due to the requirement of two carts per press and lack of space around the presses to store the carts, two mechanical carts per press were not recommended.

Mechanical Cart with Turntable. Another alternative the team investigated was the purchase of a mechanical die cart with a turntable on top that would travel on rails embedded in the floor. The cart design was proposed to span the 18-foot distance between two 500-ton presses (see **Figure 77**). It was 14 feet long, 6 feet wide, and 3 feet high. There were four push/pull arms per cart. Cart travel speed was 50 feet per minute, trolley travel was 90 feet per minute, and rotation speed was 50 feet per minute.

With the mechanical cart with turntable, the die could be loaded and unloaded from one side of the press, and die exchange could be accomplished in under three minutes. Its disadvantages were cost and overall cart size. In addition, die revision was required to use puller arms, and one cart could service only one press. Due to the overall size and lack of maneuverability, this alternative was not recommended.

Air Cart Turntable Mechanism. Using air caster technology, an air cart with a turntable mechanism was designed to float the die into position. The turntable houses two transfer arms—the die attachment system and the rotation system. With this option, die exchange could be accomplished in under two minutes. Dies could be loaded and unloaded from one side of the press, and one air cart could service multiple presses. No floor rails or shot pin floor locators were required with this alternative.

The only disadvantage found with the air cart turntable mechanism was that all cracks in the concrete floor would have to be repaired in order for the air casters to operate efficiently.

In approximately six weeks, the vendors returned to the plant and presented their proposals to the team. Based on the information gathered, the team ranked each vendor according to how well they met the project

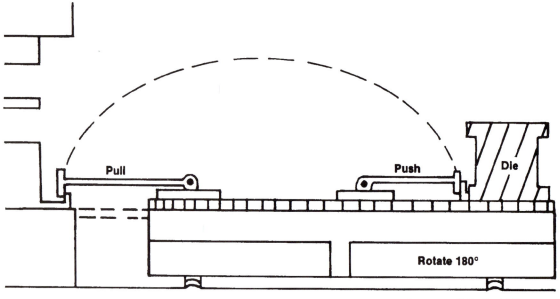

Courtesy of The Budd Company

Figure 77: Die change cart with turntable

objectives. The vendor which scored the highest total score (objective point score x vendor score = total points for that objective) became the front runner.

The team then looked at the adverse consequences of choosing the front runner over the other vendors. Once the vendor was chosen, 10 months elapsed until the equipment was shipped to the factory. The total project length from concept to installation on the factory floor was 15 months.

The Solution

The air die cart with the turntable was recommended for the quick die change program at John Deere. This die cart uses air caster technology for moving 30,000-pound die sets from the prestage die rack to the press and exchanging dies in less than two minutes.

The die handler requires only one operator, serves multiple presses, and loads and unloads from one side of the press only, in order to meet space requirements. The air cart can move in any direction and rotate with a small turning radius. Installed on the vehicle's deck is a 131-inch diameter turntable which also operates on air bearings.

Prestage. The air die cart is driven to a prestage die-ready rack and docked. A die is pulled onto one side of the vehicle's turntable deck. The cart is parked near the press prior to the job change.

Actual Die Exchange. Engagement wings on the cart and press automatically position and lock the cart to the press. When the press run is complete and the die is unbolted, the operator activates the air die rollers and extends the push/pull arm to the die. Pins to grasp the die are activated, and the arm pulls the die onto one side of the cart.

The turntable deck's air bearings are then inflated and the turntable rotates 180 degrees, bringing a new die to the press for loading. The push/pull arm pushes a new die onto the press bed. It has 65 inches of travel. The operator lowers the die by deactivating the inflatable die rollers, activates the pins to detach from the die, and returns the push/pull arm to the cart. The cart is returned to the prestage die rack for unloading.

Modifications Required

Die and press revisions were essential to accommodate the use of the air cart at both the press and the prestage die rack. Two major components that needed to be interfaced were the die rollers and engagement wings. To mount the inflatable die rollers in the bolsters, special T-slots were made. Due to the size of the bolster (60 inches by 120 inches), four die roller sections were used, providing a lifting capacity of 54,000 pounds (see **Figure 78**).

The engagement wings guide the air die cart into the proper mating position between the press and the die aboard the cart. This mating position ensures that the die is centered and parallel to the centerline of the press. When the floor air casters are deflated, the wings lock the cart to the press, ensuring that the cart will not move during a die transfer.

The die attaching system consists of two compact hydraulic cylinders located on the ends off each ram arm. The hydraulic cylinder extends and retracts the specially-designed cone-shaped rods. These rods mate and lock to the die, attaching lugs that are welded to each common subplate to assure that the die is locked to the air cart. There are two lugs on each common subplate. The cone-shaped rod self-corrects for any misalignment between the die and the ram arms. The self-correcting feature ensures repeatability of the attaching and detaching operations.

At John Deere, employee participation and management's willingness to allow their employees to try new ideas helped to make the air die cart idea became a reality.

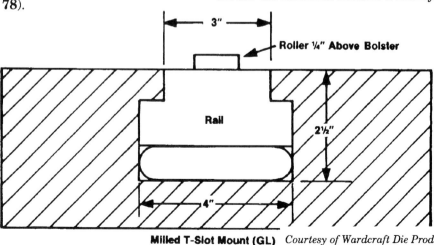

Milled T-Slot Mount (GL) *Courtesy of Wardcraft Die Products*
Patent No. 4498384

Figure 78: Die roller sections

Readying the Die Before and After Die Change

7

Providing the equipment and hardware will ensure quick die exchange, but what about all the external elements that must be addressed? Remember, to be successful, you must address all elements of time from when you stop running Part A to when you are producing a good Part B. Readying the die before and after is just as important as the die exchange itself.

Readying the Die - Before

To ready the die before the die exchange, assign manpower to ensure that the following are accomplished before the die is delivered to a die marshalling area for prestaging dies:

• A job packet (an 8-inch by 11-inch plastic folder will do) must be with each die. Certain information should be included within the packet:
    — move tickets for finished loads.
    — a part print that is clean and up to date.
    — a mechanical detail sheet showing required press adjustments, such as shut height, air pressures for cushion pins, cushion pin lengths, and die tonnage settings.

• Each die should have its own set of cushion pins with the die if cushion pins are required.
• The die must be clean.
• If major work was performed on the die, it must be tried out before delivery to the press for the production run.
• The last good piece from the previous production run should be with the die to aid the operator in first piece inspection.

Readying the Die - After

Die Maintenance. Certain procedures are crucial to ensuring that the die receives proper care after the production run. First, a tool maker assigned to the press shop inspects the bottom die and upper die shoe while in the press. He writes a work order for the die set and attaches it to the die set. Once the die is delivered to the tool room, the die repair ticket is audited and disposition of the work to be performed is determined.

The die should then be cleaned and inspected to verify the inspection ticket made out at the press. This is when a bottleneck can occur in the tool room due to the length of time required for opening and closing press dies for cleaning and maintenance. The present methods in tool rooms throughout the U.S. requires chains and hydraulic jacks to open and close press dies, and this is very time-consuming.

Die Manipulator. At a JIT factory in Wisconsin, a tool crib supervisor came up with an idea for a die manipulator. The punch presses could be changed over in under 10 minutes, but the tool room could not support them with their old die maintenance practices. At this point, employees from plant engineering services and the tool room formed a project team to identify the plant's needs and to locate possible vendors to build the equipment.

The team came up with six reasons to purchase the die manipulator:

1. **New product programs.** More existing tooling was being used for new products, and this resulted in more changeovers. In 1986, new product programs added three changeovers per week in the tool crib.

2. **Increased die inspection will be required.** The company did not have the capability to open all large tooling for inspection and washing before returning it to production.

3. **Current method is slow and cumbersome.** The present method required two people to open and close the large dies in an average time of 43 minutes. An overhead crane, chains, and hydraulic jacks were required to complete the task.

4. **Die interiors are not being washed unless it is requested by the tool room.** The space and the overhead crane was not always available for washing die interiors.

5. **Die damage.** Broken collars and leader pins were common with the present method.

6. **Safety.** There was a possibility of injury because the workers had to hammer and jump on the top of the die shoe to open and close the die. In addition, there was the possibility of broken chains on the overhead crane when rolling the top die shoe over. This had happened twice in seven years.

The old methods and equipment were not good enough to handle the increased load. The main problem was with the large dies from the 300-ton to 2,000-ton presses. Therefore, the company decided that it needed to add a piece of equipment to its tool crib to solve the problem. Once the concept was developed, it used a fact-finding trip and participative techniques for adding a die opener and a rearrangement to the tool crib.

In completing the project to purchase a new die manipulator, the project manager followed the necessary steps:

- Develop a plan of action
- Assemble a project team
- Develop a machine specification
- Select a vendor
- Build and install the machine

Plan of Action. The first step was to organize the project by developing a plan of action (see **Figure 79**). The plan of action puts all the key elements of the project together. It helps determine the manpower and time required to investigate the various equipment alternatives and provides a means by which the project manager can understand all the pieces of the puzzle.

Project Team. Following the second step, the project manager assembled representatives from production, maintenance, and the tool crib to form a project team. The team members (shown below) were responsible for developing the design and machine specifications and selecting the vendor:

- Project manager (process and tool)   1
- Plant engineer   1
- Industrial engineer   1
- Crib supervisors   2
- Hourly personnel (tool room)   2
- Hourly personnel (tool crib)   9
- Hourly personnel (maintenance mechanic)   1

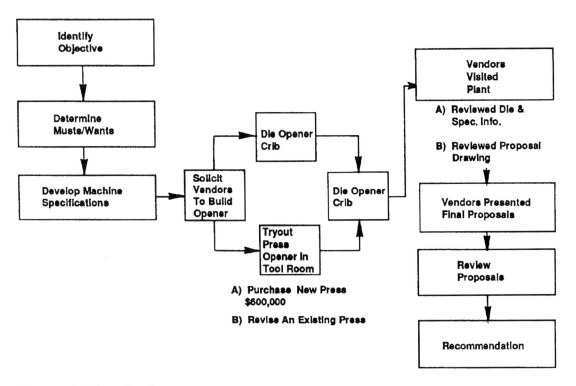

Figure 79: Plan of action

This team included employees from all levels in the plant, allowing everyone who would be affected by the purchase of the die manipulator to provide input on decisions.

Machine Specification. Once the concept was developed, participative techniques and fact-finding trips were used to develop machine specifications (see **Figure 80**). However, the die manipulator had to be able to automatically open, rotate, and close large press dies for changeover and washing. Feedback from the fact-finding trips showed that there was no equipment available in the U.S. or overseas that would meet the company's requirements. Therefore, it decided to select a U.S. machine builder to design and build a one-of-a-kind die manipulator to the company's specifications.

Vendor. In the search for a vendor, the company evaluated the following alternatives:

• Die opener/tryout press
• Conventional die opener
• New state-of-the-art combination of die cart/gantry for opening/closing dies.

Before the equipment specifications could be finalized, a decision had to be made about whether the new equipment belonged in the crib or the tool room. The company's tool room was, for years, trying to justify a new tryout press to spot dies following die

Die Opener - Machine Specification

Automatically open and close die push button control

Automatically align top and bottom shoe in opener

Adjustable rails on both top and bottom of opener
(with T-slots) - Removable (4 each - bottom)
          (6 each - top)

Die rollers (Ward Craft Conv.) mounted on bottom
of opener (4 roller sections)

Rotate top die shoe 180° automatically

Top of opener must be accessible to use overhead crane

Automatically aside bottom shoe after die is opened
  A) Motor driven cart/rail system
  B) Longitudinal travel

Rotate bottom die shoe 100° outside of die opener

Capacity
  Max. die wt.   35,000 lbs.
  Max. top shoe wt. 20,000 lbs.
  Max. die length   140" R-L
  Max. die width   72" F-B
  Min. shut height   4"
  Total opening   54"
  Stroke   50"
  Recommended
   working height   30"

Controls
  2-speeds to open/close die
  Inch mode to fine tune alignment
  Soft start
  Pendant controls (3)
    A) Each side of opener
    B) Cart

Wash Dies
  Drip through walkways to aside grime, water, and dirt
  Moisture-proof controls

Drive Mechanism
  Rotate top shoe - Worm gear drive
  Lift and lower top
  Die shoe - Electric powered driven ball screws
     with boots

Die positioning on cart - locating pins to center die on
cart - use v-notch die lead on existing subplates

Scrappers on FRT & RR of cart to aside slugs from track

Alignment Tolerances
  Levelness = ± .020" Opposite corners

Figure 80: Die opener—machine specification

polishing or major repairs. The only piece of equipment known to the company to perform this task was in Japan. A 500-ton hydraulic press was similar to a standard tryout press with a sliding bolster, except that the ram tilted 90 degrees for access to the top die shoe (see **Figure 81**). The press bed measured 120 inches right to left and 72 inches front to back. It had two 150-ton cushions, with a 10-inch stroke on each cushion.

Although it could open and close 100 percent of all press tooling and its die tryouts caused less press downtime, the disadvantages (including problems with job classification, space, labor, and layout) convinced the team not to recommend the press. Instead, the best decision at the time was to purchase a new piece of equipment to be located in the tool

Tilt Ram 90°

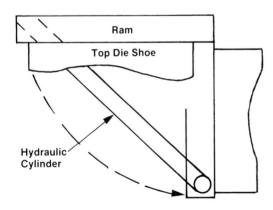

Figure 81: Die opener—tryout press

crib for die cleaning and inspections. The anticipated return on the investment was estimated at 2.7 years (see **Figure 82**).

Another option that the team evaluated was to have a major producer of small conventional die openers (less than 8,000-pound capacity) build this equipment. After several months of consultation, the producer's proposal was received. The producer recommended altering its standard unit, but this was unacceptable. Although it would rotate the top die shoe 180 degrees, the major disadvantage of this proposal was that after the die was opened, the bottom die shoe would have to be asided and repositioned manually. After reviewing all of the advantages and disadvantages, the project team decided not to recommend the conventional die opener.

Three vendors were invited to the factory at different dates and given the machine specifications and a plant tour. Following a tour, they met with the project team and reviewed the objectives with them. These objectives were rated for importance (10 = highest, 1 = lowest):

- Accessibility to the die once it is opened for changeover and washing — 10
- Minimized total changeover time — 10
- Capability to open all variations of the die presently in house — 9
- Ability to add or remove die from subplate with a hoist or die truck — 8
- Capability to perform clearance checks — 7
- Ability to rotate bottom die shoe 90 degrees — 5
- Potential for asiding dies during lag time — 5
- Serviceability for preventive maintenance — 4

93

Justification for Die Opener

A.   **Tangible Savings**

   1) **Reduce Labor Cost To Open and Close Press Dies**

	Avg./Day Present	Avg./Day Proposes With JIT
Open/Close Dies To Wash or Changeover	9	18

   Present Method 43 Mins./Cycle (1.5 People)

   Proposed   20 Mins./Cycle (1.5 People)

   Projected Yearly Savings   **$43,400**

   2) **Repair Tooling In Tool Room For Broken Collars and Leader Pins**

	Yearly Cost
Material	$ 3,000
Labor	**$12,000**
Total	$15,000

B.   **Projected Return On Investment**

Cost For Die Opener	$152,000	
	———	= 2.7 Years Pay Back
Total Yearly Savings	$ 58,000	

C.   **Intangible Savings**

   * Improved Safety - We no longer have to jump and hammer on the top die shoe to open and close dies

   * Improved Part Quality - More time can now be spent for cleaning and inpecting tooling. This will reduce die marks caused by dirt and oil deposits in the die.

Figure 82: Justification for die opener

- Requirement for minimum
  amount of hoist use   2
- Ease of operation of equipment   2
- Minimized space   1

In approximately six weeks, the vendors were asked to return to the company's plant to present their proposals to the team. Based on the information gathered, the team then ranked each vendor according to how well they met its objectives. The vendor which scored the highest point total (objective point score x the vendor score = total points for that objective) for all nine objectives became the front runner. The team then considered the adverse consequences of going with the front runner versus the other vendors. Once the vendor was chosen, 10 months elapsed until the equipment was shipped to the factory.

Summary. Total project length from concept to installation on the factory floor was 15 months. Two months were spent in de-veloping the concept, three months passed while the team selected a vendor, and 10 months were spent in building and installing the machine.

The basic operation of a die manipulator (see **Figure 83**) involves a number of steps. The die is loaded onto the cart via a die set truck. Ball bearings in parallels reduce friction during the load cycle and die positioning. The die is fastened to T-slot parallels in the conventional manner using air impact wrenches. The upper platen is lowered and fastened in the same manner as the lower half. Time for one person to clamp and unclamp the top and bottom die shoes is 10 minutes.

The upper platen is raised approximately 40 inches to clear the lower die. The lower die cart traverses out from the gantry traveling approximately 15 feet on rails and train-type wheels to the wash booth. In the wash booth, the die is rotated to a 90-degree position for inspection and washing. The wash consists of a standard water hose and standard city water

Figure 83: Die manipulator

Courtesy of Planet Corporation

pressure. The water base drawing compound is easily removed with just hot water. No other solvents or detergents are required to clean the dies.

The upper half of the die within the gantry is rotated 90 degrees on the trunnion mount for inspection and washing. The wash area is open on all four sides and the cement floor is sloped to a drain at one end, approximately 60 feet.

After washing, both die halves are inspected, and die repair taking less than one hour is performed as required. The lower die is returned under the gantry and both halves are aligned in the normal position. The upper die is then lowered onto the lower half and the operator unfastens the hold-down bolts. The die is removed from the gantry by a die set truck operated by the same employee doing the washing and inspection. The whole sequence of die open, wash, and die close takes approximately 23 minutes.

The die separator is equipped with safety devices (hydraulic cylinder shot pins) to prevent rotation of the die shoe during wash or inspection modes. These cylinders are normally closed with spring pressure and retracted with hydraulic pressure during the rotate cycle.

Since the start-up of the die opener, the company has identified many benefits. Short term die maintenance (one hour or less) can now be done in the die opener. Repairs such as replacing the stripper bolts and locators, polishing form steels, grinding and shimming die blocks, and refurbishing form blocks are now completed while the die halves are separated in the opener. The interior of each individual large press die can now be cleaned once a month instead of once every four months, as it was before the die opener was purchased. As a result of routine inspections,

potential die problems are now being discovered. They included chipped die blocks, broken stripper bolts and springs, and wear on form die blocks. These problems were found on dies returning from production runs with no wire up for die maintenance.

Sharing of the 25-ton crane by both the tool room and the tool crib is no longer required. As a result, 6.0 hours have been freed up for tool room use. In addition, actual labor savings have exceeded expectations. The projected amounts were for a yearly labor savings of $43,400 in opening and closing dies. The actual yearly labor savings are $48,000 in opening and closing dies, and $23,000 in trucking. The labor savings in trucking were seen because the die opener allowed the tool crib to change die handling procedures, resulting in minimum time for transporting tools.

Before the opener was purchased, workers had to move the die to the wash booth and wash the die exterior; move the die from the wash booth to the tool crib; move the die from storage to the tool room for die opening; truck the die halves to wash the booth; truck each die half from the wash booth to the tool room; and truck the closed die to storage. Since the die opener has been implemented, workers need only to move the die to the gantry, load the cart, and then unload the die from the cart and aside it to storage. So, the total number of die handlings has been reduced from seven to two. The end result, as seen above, is a greatly reduced die trucking time and indirect labor savings.

With these trucking savings added to the labor savings in opening and closing the dies, the actual payback time for purchasing the die manipulator was seen to be 2.2 years at the company, rather than the estimated 2.7 years.

Due to employee participation and management's foresight to allow their employees to try new ideas, the die manipulator became a reality. Historically, the tool cribs and tool rooms throughout American press shops are the last place anyone hears about productivity improvements. As a result of JIT manufacturing, problems arising in the tool crib were turned into an opportunity for faster, less costly operations.

Conclusion

Reflecting on what has been said, the book has covered the hardware, methods and equipment alternatives any project manager must consider in evaluating any quick die change project. As the data show, this is no easy task.

A number of companies who have attempted to implement quick die change have failed. Upon looking at these companies, a number of similar problems become apparent. In each case:

• **A project manager was not selected and given full-time responsibility.** Instead, the project was approached with a minimum amount of time and energy. To be effective, time and energy must be spent putting it together. In quick die change implementations, planning is most crucial. Because of the equipment choices and the size and cost of such a project, a project manager must be selected for full-time work on the implementation.

• **The project was not implemented correctly.** Not all tooling on the press was standardized for quick die change, and many dies were not ready to be used with the quick die change system when installed. The end result was that the quick die change hardware was damaged when non-quick-changed dies were run on that press.

For example, a company in Ohio implemented quick die change on one 400-ton press. After installing rollers and clamping, the company continued to use a fork truck for die exchange. The fork truck tore out some of the hoses for hydraulic clamps several weeks after they were installed. Die rollers were also damaged until they could no longer function correctly.

To be successful, all dies must be standardized on the press and the die handling system selected. The environment in which the die handling system is to function must be fitted to the die cart system.

• **No commitment was given by top management.** Because of the magnitude of a quick die change project, large amounts of time and manpower are needed. If top management is not willing to give support, the project will fail.

This book has covered some of the hardware and equipment improvements from the early 1980s to 1990 that the author has used. There are many new innovations, and the future of quick die change is exciting as it promotes further new innovations. The author is presently involved in the start-up of three new quick die change handling systems using wheeled vehicles for die exchange. These vehicles allow the customer to exchange dies quickly (two minutes) and service multiple presses, without concerns for floor modifications, which is a constant problem with air cart design.

As we continue to make improvements in how we manufacture, we must not lose sight of the customer we are trying to service. That customer is the press operator. It is our job as engineers to make his job simpler, safer, and to provide him with a better environment in which to work. The end result will be improved employee morale, higher production, and a better quality product.

If we establish these goals as our engineering goals in pursuing quick die change, we will be successful and America will be successful.

About the Author

Gary Zunker is president of Lightning Time Savers, a consulting firm which specializes in quick-change hardware and methods improvement. He has aided clients in the agriculture, lawn and garden, automotive, aerospace, and electronic components industries.

Prior to consulting, Mr. Zunker managed the John Deere-Horicon quick change program. During his five years at Horicon, job change standards were reduced from 130 minutes to under 10 minutes. New innovations in technology implemented while he was in their employment included: a fully automatic die cart exchange system; and a die manipulator first built in the U.S. to automatically open and close large dies for maintenance and cleaning.

He has conducted seminars sponsored by the University of Wisconsin - Milwaukee throughout the U.S. and Canada. He also addressed the second world conference on Just-In-Time at London, England, on the subject of die handling.

His company is presently coordinating press quick change retrofits for the Boeing New Plant of the Future in Seattle, Washington; helping with the revitalization of Navistar's existing press plant in Springfield, Ohio; and aiding the development of the John Deere tractor facility for Just-In-Time (JIT) manufacturing in Waterloo, Iowa.

In addition, Mr. Zunker is working closely with Aero-Go, a builder of die cart systems, in designing a new, state-of-the-art

line of fully steerable-drive wheeled vehicles for exchanging dies with weights from 4,000 to 100,000 pounds.

Mr. Zunker has 18 years of experience in manufacturing engineering. He has held a variety of positions, including industrial engineer, shop floor general supervisor, and supervisor of both industrial and process and tool engineering departments. He is an experienced "shirt sleeve" worker in both a job shop and mass production plant environment.

Mr. Zunker has degrees in business administration from the University of Wisconsin at Oshkosh and has done postgraduate work at the University of West Virginia.

He was awarded the 1986 Fabricating Industry Award of Excellence from the Fabricators and Manufacturers Association International for his work in designing an innovative die changing system for stamping presses.

References

[1] "Shedding no tears for USA; Japanese politician lectures 'giant crybaby'; U.S. audience angered but also agrees," <u>USA TODAY</u> 21 May, 1990. Copyright 1990, USA TODAY. Excerpted with permission.

[2] Morita, Akio and Shintaro Ishihara, <u>The Japan That Can Say "No"</u>. Washington, D.C.: U.S. Government Printing Office, 1989.

[3] Enerpac Production Automation, Butler, Wisconsin.

[4] Enerpac Production Automation, Butler, Wisconsin.

[5] Atlas Technologies, Inc., Fenton, Michigan.

[6] Zunker, Gary. "Innovative, Quick Die Change Air Cart." <u>STAMPING Quarterly</u>® Fall 1989: 40-44.

Index